# The Marketing Person's
## Guide to
# DATABASE MARKETING
# &
# DIRECT MAIL

# The Marketing Person's Guide to

## DATABASE MARKETING

## & DIRECT MAIL

## ROBIN FAIRLIE

**EXLEY**

First published in Great Britain 1990 by
Exley Publications Ltd, 16 Chalk Hill, Watford,
Herts. WD1 4BN

**British Library Cataloguing in Publication Data**
Fairlie, Robin
   Database marketing.
    1. Business firms. Marketing. Applications of
     computer systems. Machine-readable files.
   I. Title.
   658.8'0028'574

**ISBN 1-85015-209-8**

Typeset by Brush Off Studios, St Albans.
Printed and bound in Great Britain by
Billing & Sons Ltd, Worcester.

# Contents

# Introduction

This book is about the two interlinked – but independent – concepts of database marketing and direct mail. There is a tendency in some quarters to confuse the two. The development of direct mail, and its growing use by business houses, has been a long, slow process, extending now over three generations. While the use of the postal services by businesses to communicate with customers or prospects is at least as old as the Post Office itself, the actual development of today's direct mail industry can be said to have started in the USA in the early 1900s. Yet the industry on both sides of the Atlantic is only now reaching maturity with the conscious involvement, for the first time, of the majority of business houses with the medium – and indeed with its discovery by charities, by churches, and by political parties.

Database, by contrast, was a concept born of the computer industry in the 1960s; it has hit the business world with the impact to be expected from the offspring of such parentage. Suddenly a term, coined only twenty odd years ago, and rarely heard then outside the more esoteric computer seminars, is on everyone's lips, and every computer user possessed of a handful of names and addresses is either claiming to have a database or wondering how to acquire one.

For marketing people in general, and direct mail users in particular, concerned about how to obtain and use more, and more reliable, information about increasingly fragmented markets, database seems like the answer to a prayer. We are approaching the time when every serious marketing department will have a database, and when every user of a marketing database will be a user also of direct mail, whether as a primary or a secondary way of maximizing the value of his investment in information. So where does the one discipline end, and the other begin?

Direct mail is simply the sending of business communications to individual persons through the post. Database marketing means using information about individual persons in such a way as to improve the effectiveness of one's marketing techniques – whether these techniques happen to use direct mail or some other medium.

In practice, of course, if one has substantial information of marketing relevance about named individuals (which normally includes their addresses) it would seem natural to use the postal services to establish and maintain some kind of link with these persons. But there are alternatives: one can use the information available to enhance the efforts of a sales force, or of a telephone marketing service, for example.

Moreover, the uses of database are not confined to selecting individuals to whom communications can be made, whether through the post or by other means. The opportunities offered by good database facilities for analysis of information, for example, so as to give new insights into markets, are immense. Database techniques, then, offer a means of defining and refining markets. Direct mail is one major medium through which markets so defined can be exploited.

So, the subjects of our interest do exist independently, and we will look at them, at least initially, each in turn. The excuse for dealing with both between one set of covers is simply that it is hard to envisage a database user not being moved, at some point, to use direct mail – even though that may not have been the original motivation in building a database. Similarly, most users of direct mail, if they are to use the medium effectively by targeting their promotions to qualified prospects, will increasingly have to consider database techniques as a way of giving them access to a necessary knowledge of their prospects' needs.

In old-fashioned business circles you will still hear direct mail referred to (when mentioned at all) as an advertising medium. It is not. Direct mail is a marketing medium; advertising is one function of marketing, and one function, therefore, of direct mail. Direct mail is, in turn, one arm of marketing – an arm whose muscle power is provided by information, such as can be held and ordered by database techniques.

In the beginning there were two kinds of companies – the direct mail companies and the rest. (I had almost said Reader's Digest and everybody else.) For the former, direct mail was a total way of life; for the latter it didn't exist. Those who used the medium, used it to advertise, to conduct market research, and to sell – the three classic marketing functions. And they used little or nothing else. Everybody else preferred not to know.

Those days have gone, on both sides. Reader's Digest itself now advertises on hoardings, in the press, on television and sells its wares through retail outlets as well as by mail. And the rest of the world is learning rapidly, even with some enthusiasm, to use direct mail – not in the old way, as an all-purpose, or exclusive, device, but as one limb in a total integrated marketing strategy, deriving strength from, and contributing to, other forms of marketing activity.

So, what has caused this change, and is it likely to continue? In part, of course, it's a bandwagon effect, but that begs the real question – what started the bandwagon rolling in the first place? The largest single factor would seem to be the growing fragmentation of the consumer market, which makes it necessary for marketers to target their efforts ever more precisely. Improved targeting has rather limited scope in the traditional media; nor has direct mail, with its mass marketing approach, always been as outstanding in this regard as its public apologists would like us to think. But direct mail does contain within itself the *possibility* of close targeting, and it is significant that as the roll-call of its users grows, so the development of more highly selective tools gathers pace. This can be seen in the growing use of demographics, and the collection of life-style data – as well as the development of database techniques (all of which we will be considering later in this book).

A second factor of major importance has been the year-by-year change in relative cost-performance of the different media. In 1986/7 the average cost of postage per piece of direct mail was 14p – compared with 12.6p in 1981/2: an increase of 11%, far below the rate of inflation for the period. Unfortunately there is no comparable set of figures for the average cost of a minute of air-time, or a column-inch in the press, but no one could dispute that if such figures were available, they would show a much steeper increase. The Post Office has done much in the last ten years to encourage direct mail growth, but its most important contribution by far has been to keep price increases to a minimum.

A further factor has been the explosion in financial services in the mid-80s, symbolized by the Big Bang in the City of London in 1986. During this period powerful financial institutions, with ample resources, found themselves quite suddenly faced with having to market an immensely widened range of services – and with a ready-made market for those services in the shape of lists of existing customers for their traditional range.

And finally one must refer to the general perception of the direct mail industry – both by those who are daily exposed to its blandishments, and by those who are considering using it for the first time. Overall there can be no doubt that this image is improving – from a very low base, be it said. The improvement is in part due to the influx of new users, many of them well-known and respected names in the market-place; in part it is due to the efforts made by the industry itself to clean up its act. The work of the Mailing Preference Service, the Direct Mail Services Standards Board, and the Direct

Mail Sales Bureau have all contributed to this improved perception.

This book is addressed, as its title suggests, to marketing staff, regardless of the particular marketing discipline in which they may have been raised. And to those marketing staff, especially, who have learned, or recognized, or sensed, that to run a marketing department in the 1990s without reference to direct mail will be rather like trying to walk on one leg: it can be done, but at some cost in efficiency of locomotion. We do not aim to instruct the reader in how to become a direct mail expert, or in how to build a database. There is nothing here on how to write sales letters, or other forms of copy, nor on sampling theory or production methods, or legal obligations. Nor do we deal with the technical distinctions between hierarchical, network, and relational databases. For those who want, or need, to get involved in such matters there is a sufficiency of books already; some are listed in the Bibliography.

Rather we seek first to suggest what it is that newcomers to these techniques might look for by way of assistance to their existing marketing efforts. And having discussed what is on offer, we then discuss how best to obtain it – using in the first instance the services of others. Using direct mail, or running a database, can be an activity for an expert – and a very fascinating one too. But it needn't be. There is, within the direct marketing industry, every kind of service house offering the advertiser every kind of service, at different levels of cost and expertise. To use such service houses to best advantage requires some knowledge, and the exercise of some management skills. That is what this book seeks to provide – a basic collection of do's and don'ts for those who employ direct marketing agencies or computer bureaux, and a guide through the jungle of service houses to enable them to exercise intelligent choice in determining which are likely to be best, or least, able to meet particular needs.

Our first chapter, then, deals with direct mail, and our second and third with database, while four to six might be held relevant to a discussion of either. The remainder of the book deals with services which a user in either field may require, and how to find and utilize them to best advantage.

# 1 Direct Mail in an Integrated Marketing Strategy

In this chapter we will consider the use of the direct mail medium in advertising, in selling and in market research. In each context we will consider how the medium can be used to reinforce other parallel efforts.

## 1 Advertising

The early pioneers of direct mail, who built a living on the medium, thought of it as a means of selling products for distribution through the mail. The fact that it also performed an advertising function at the same time was, to them, incidental, irrelevant, and even unrecognized. The point can be illustrated by an interesting (and true) story. As late as the early 1960s Reader's Digest – till then basically a magazine publishing house – started to produce hardback non-fiction titles for sale by direct mail. These sold well, and pretty soon some bright young man thought it would be a good idea to sell a few copies through the bookshops also. The real object of this exercise was not directly to maximize the sale of books, but to enable Reader's Digest, by pricing books for retail sale at a higher level than direct mail copies, to claim a "saving" for its direct mail purchasers.

The outcome was a considerable surprise: Reader's Digest books sold through bookshops, despite the higher price, like hot cakes, in numbers that greatly outstripped the expectations not only of Reader's Digest staff – amateurs in the retail business – but of Hodder and Stoughton, the experienced traditional publishers who had undertaken trade distribution of the titles. Book after book, and year after year the story went on. At last the penny dropped. When Reader's Digest promoted a book by direct mail, an elaborate promotion shot went through anything from one to two million letterboxes. Orders would be received, from a large number (but still quite a small percentage) of those promoted. The company made a profit, and was well satisfied. But what of the great majority of promotees who had not replied? Nobody thought, or much cared, about them. Yet they had been exposed, in large numbers, to an *advertisement.* Much more directly exposed, indeed, than if they had merely been buyers of a newspaper in which an advertisement had appeared. And those of them that walked into a bookshop a week, or a month, later, looking, say, for a cookery book, might see on the shelf a book, perhaps in the cookery section, somewhat familiar in appearance. That was the one they would take first...and probably buy...

What was being seen in this unexpected way was the power of advertising to condition, and help to persuade. And it was being seen by a company which, at least until then, and indeed for some years afterwards, maintained a decidedly ambivalent attitude to "mere" advertising, being happy to sell space in its magazine to others, but highly dubious of the efficacy of the activity for its own purposes. (Of course the effect was heightened by the fact that very few books then, or now, are advertised to the buying public to any notable extent at all. How publishers, leave alone booksellers, expect to make a living at their peculiar trade is altogether beyond me.)

Those for whom advertising is a way of life – in particular the major advertising agencies – have been, until very recent times, at least equally blind. Some still are. How can a major motor car manufacturer, to take an example, continue to pour money into expensive, and largely undirected, advertisements on television and in the colour supplements, while failing to correspond on an individual and personal level with its own *known* customers? It is, I suppose, only to be expected that the first two car companies to see the light should have been overseas manufacturers whose UK operations are not burdened by British management on a large scale – Volvo and Toyota.

Yet it is the advertising agencies, rather than the advertiser, with whom the blame for years of lost opportunities must first lie. The reasons for this state of affairs are various, and worth pondering:

a) Direct mail isn't "glamorous". Trendy young account executives, copy-writers, visualizers, are unlikely to feel that their favoured lifestyle, which revolves round TV studios, models, fashionable photographers, and exotic locations, is enhanced by anything so square and every-day as direct mail. So, from top to bottom of every advertising agency there is a hard core of those who don't want to know about anything that is outside the mainstream of their preferred experience.

b) Worse still, direct mail is – or is held to be – hard work. Knowledge is required, if a client is to be properly advised in the medium, of a kind that main-line agency personnel don't have. And there is still little facility, inside or outside the agencies, for teaching the art, or science, of direct mail to those that do want to find out.*

c) More: when one masterminds a TV and/or press campaign for a client there is normally one, and only one, crunch point – does the client like it? In direct mail there is – or should be if the medium is properly used – another and much more objective test: what is the measurable response, and what has it cost to get that response? There is, of course, good advertising to be seen on television, on poster sites, and in the press. Some of it even produces some quantifiable results, from which it can, by and large, be adjudged a success. There is also a great deal of very poor advertising, which is almost certainly a waste, partial or total, of the advertiser's money. But so long as the client is satisfied, and the agency gets its commission, who knows, or cares? Direct mail, by contrast, has this unpleasant knack of identifying winners and losers; nobody, who doesn't have to, is anxious to put their head on the chopping block every time a mailing goes out.

d) Finally, direct mail doesn't fit conveniently into the agency's financial scheme. An agency handling a client's press campaign gets its reward from the 15% commission allowed by the medium on the cost of space booked. In direct mail the medium "owner" is, if you will, the Post Office. And although the Post Office has changed a great deal in the last 15 years, and offers a whole range of rebates, discounts, special terms and services to encourage use of the post, all of these are available, not to the agency (to whom the Post Office is not, or not yet, in the business of offering a commission) but to the ultimate advertiser. So, if the client is knowledgeable enough, and brave enough, to insist on having direct mail included in the schedule, the creative cost must either be carried by the agency as an unwanted overhead, or, contrary to practice with other media, a basis must be found for charging a fee to the client.

Change is coming, with all the heady, exciting speed of a glacier rushing downhill to the sea – but also with some of its inevitability. The most hoity-toity of agencies can't forever go on ignoring the fastest-growing source of advertising in the business. So there are

---

* The Direct Marketing Centre, 1 Park Road, Teddington, Middlesex, is the industry's first attempt (set up in 1987) to create a broad educational facility.

now not only a few agencies that specialize in direct mail, and that operate (without the world coming to an end) on a fee basis; there are also direct marketing arms, or subsidiaries, of most of the main-line agencies, created in the last few years in an attempt to jump, late in the day, on the direct mail bandwagon before it accelerates out of sight.

So far, these direct marketing subsidiaries are still sitting not only "below the line" but also well below the salt, as far as the parent agency personnel are concerned, but this may not last. The whole idea of having a direct marketing subsidiary is itself a fairly pathetic attempt to solve the problem caused by the ignorance of most agency personnel of an important branch of their trade. Pathetic, because it attempts to answer yesterday's problem of how to provide a service for those who wish to advertise by direct mail, without addressing today's problem – which is how to provide an *integrated* multi-media advertising service to clients who want to co-ordinate their activity across all forms of outlet. Any advertiser looking for a new agency today would do well to seek out an agency that can offer, within a single organization structure, skills across the board. There are not too many of them about, and they aren't today's big names either. Their turn will come.

So, what are the advertising functions that this medium, ignored for so long by the main-line agencies, can be expected to perform for the advertiser? Clearly, the primary function of any advertisement is to deliver a message to those people the advertiser wishes to address. This function we must consider in two parts. First, as to conveying a message, it is plain that direct mail is well-equipped – its centre-piece being that oldest of all devices for the purpose, namely a letter. Secondly, there is the question of the audience to be addressed – what the direct mail industry has traditionally referred to as the list. Here direct mail has a potential advantage over all other media. There is no way, using newspaper, television, radio, poster advertising, in which a message can be delivered to all the people and only the people that the advertiser wishes to reach – achieving maximum impact and optimum economy at one and the same time. To be honest, there are not that many direct mail campaigns that come close to this ideal either – but the possibility is there. An advertiser, or an agency working on the advertiser's behalf, may well be able to compile a list of precisely those people, and no one else, likely to be interested in this product or service. No newspaper or collection of newspapers can offer such a profile. And if they could, a high proportion of those "reached" in this way would never see the advertisement.

As we shall see later on, it is in this whole area of list compilation that we move from the first subject matter of this book – direct mail – to its second – database. The traditional direct mail list is a fairly static entity, consisting of names and addresses and a minimal quantity of information about the source of the said names. A database is a dynamic affair, where the information stored changes continually; it enables its owner to keep day-by-day track of changes in the market-place. Database techniques bring closer to reality the dream of being able to achieve perfect targeting for one's advertising message.

Next, an advertisement, having delivered a message, must persuade at least a proportion of those reached. Persuade them to hold, or change, or modify, a view, or to remember something – a name, or a fact – or to act in a certain way. As a persuader, direct mail has a number of advantages; above all it is not pressed for time. The reader of a newspaper or magazine advertisement is, ten to one, trying to get to the leader page before the coffee gets cold, and glances impatiently at intervening advertisement headlines, anxious to move on. The television camera, burning hundred pound notes as the motor turns, dare not linger. Direct mail moves at a more leisurely pace. Newspaper and television advertising is, for most of its audience, an intrusion on the true purpose of the medium in which it appears – an irrelevance at best, an impertinence at worst. Direct mail advertising stands, or falls, on its own.

Finally, an advertisement, having reached the right parties, or some of them, and having persuaded a proportion to the end desired by the advertiser, must be cost-effective. Or must be believed to be so. Indeed, this last criterion really embraces the other two as well: an advertiser can, eventually, reach the whole of a chosen audience by dint of repeated saturation coverage in any one medium or media-mix. And the campaign can be marvellously persuasive if time and/or space are no problem. But cost is likely to run riot. Direct mail doesn't avoid these problems, but it is remarkably adept at minimizing them. A sharply-profiled list avoids the cost of advertising to parties devoid of interest in your subject. The medium itself, by being directly addressable to individual persons by name ensures the best possible chance that the material will be seen, and read, by those to whom it is addressed – thus minimizing the wasted cost of material that is never seen. The cost of each extra hundred words of persuasion, each additional illustration, is tiny: 60 grams (the basic postal weight step) is a whole lot of paper.

But most important of all is the fact that direct mail is a response-oriented medium, and because it has this facility, it is possible to measure and evaluate the effects of a direct mail campaign, as of few others. And thus to know if it was cost-effective, and at what

level. Of course, any advertisement in any medium can invite response – even radio or television. But no other medium (except the
telephone) makes it so easy as direct mail. So much so that we may
safely lay it down that the first and cardinal sin in the use of direct
mail is to send out material that does *not* demand a response.

So, a direct mail advertisement must be a verifiably cost-effective
way of delivering a persuasive message to a chosen audience. And
in order to do that properly, any direct mail shot must contain these
elements:

a) a letter. A direct mail shot without a letter is like a car body
without an engine – it will get you nowhere. It is still truly remark-
able how many such shots get sent out.

b) a response medium which the addressee can return to indicate
whatever type of response the advertiser is seeking – or just to
indicate the effect of the promotion overall.

At a less essential level, most direct mail shots also contain:

c) an outer envelope or wrapping. But it is possible to have an
all-in-one self-mailer which dispenses with this item.

And sometimes:

d) a leaflet, to give a more visually-dramatic impact to the offer.

e) a reply envelope, pre-addressed and pre-paid; this should only
be dispensed with where the response medium is itself a reply
card which can be dropped straight in the letter box, or some kind
of self-mailer device.

To which can be added as many others as the imagination can devise.

Armed with these items, what types of persuasion can a direct
mail advertisement seek to exert? It is common to think of direct
mail in two distinct categories – business mail, which is addressed
by one business house to another – or to individual persons in their
business or professional capacities; consumer mail, which is addressed by a business house to individual members of the public at their
private homes. It is true that in some significant respects the two
types of approach are different – but not in all respects. So, for
example, direct mail, whether business or consumer, can be used to:

a) **Qualify prospects** The principle here is the same in either case.

For example, a company dealing direct with consumers may wish to send a heavy, expensive catalogue to a substantial number of really good prospects – but to avoid the considerable cost of sending it to numbers of people who are not really interested. So a first direct mail shot will go to a large audience, seeking to elicit a response only from those who will be interested in buying from the catalogue. This is the kind of operation that the mail order houses – GUS, Littlewoods, Grattans – undertake in looking for "agents". Alternatively, a sales manager may wish to determine which business houses in a given area are worth the time of a salesman in making a call. Every year salesmen's time becomes more expensive in real terms; direct mail (whose largest single cost element is postage) has tended for some years past to become cheaper. Consequently, the use of direct mail to persuade businessmen to identify themselves as good, or less good, prospects, can turn a team of salesmen into a very much more productive and cost-effective unit. (Note, please, that it is no part of our contention that direct mail can substitute for, or replace, a sales team; the two operate quite differently, and have different strengths and weaknesses. Here, as elsewhere, the emphasis should be on the use of direct mail to complement and enhance other sales and marketing efforts, not to replace them.) And, as we shall see, the harnessing of database techniques to an integrated system, employing both salesmen and direct mail, gives an even sharper cutting edge to a company's efforts.

Again, direct mail can be used to:

**b) Supply information** – perhaps to a customer list (of business people or consumers) about a new product or service. This of course is the type of information the marketer most often wants to impart. But it is worth pausing for a moment to ask what kind of information the customer most wants to receive. For example, if you bought a new Volvo last year from your local dealer, would you be more impressed by a letter from the company's sales director extolling the superior merits of this year's model, or by a polite letter from your local dealer reminding you that your car is due for servicing in two weeks' time, and offering you an appointment (with, of course, a brochure about the new model enclosed)?

Here too it should be remembered that, even where the supply of information is the major marketing objective, direct mail should not be a one-way street; it is important to have the addressee respond, because only so can one measure the effectiveness with which information has been conveyed.

Or to:

c) **Distribute samples** It should be remembered that, while a letter is a necessary part of any direct mail shot, it is not the only possible component, and that things other than words and pictures on paper can be conveyed by mail. This characteristic again sets it apart from other media.

There is a multitude of particular functions that a direct mail advertisement (considered only as an advertisement, not as a sales medium) can be called on to perform; most of them can probably be subsumed under one of these headings – the qualifying of prospects, the conveying of information, the distribution of samples. (And of these functions, the traditional advertising media can offer equivalent if different advantages in only one – the conveying of information.) Too many advertisements – regardless of the medium they use – fail because the advertiser has not begun by asking two vital questions: what, precisely, is to be accomplished with this advertisement, and what kind of message is the intended audience likely to listen to. It is only when these questions have been answered that it becomes relevant to ask which particular medium – or mix of media – is best qualified to achieve the stated objective.

## 2 Selling

The use of mixed media becomes an even more interesting possibility when the objective is not simply to advertise a product or service, but to sell it. The combined use of television and direct mail contains some interesting examples: a well-known television personality will be used to advise viewers that they may be the lucky recipients, next day by post, of an exciting new offer, which they should be sure to read and deal with straight away. This approach combines the strengths of the two media instructively: the TV spot creates interest and a point of recognition for those who receive the mailing (or a proportion of them, since not all will have seen the TV advertisement). The announcer, if well-chosen, lends the reassurance of his familiar personality to the necessarily impersonal mailshot.

It is a curious fact that consumers appear to regard television as a more credible and trustworthy source of advertising information than other media, even when the same information is being conveyed by each. This has, perhaps, something to do with the use in television of people with faces and voices, where the print media have only silent pictures, and the written word. It is also, sadly, the case that direct mail is widely regarded as the least trustworthy of the media; the effect of reinforcement by television is therefore to lend it a greater credibility than it would otherwise achieve. Then again, television has its weaknesses:

a) Time is short – complex messages can't be conveyed;

b) Television is not a response-oriented medium – viewers are not sitting in large numbers with pencils poised ready to jot down reply addresses;

c) The message, once delivered, is retained only as a memory in the viewer's mind, not as a physical document that can be referred to again.

Direct mail's strengths lie in just those areas: the medium can convey whatever complexity of message the advertiser desires, with minimum impact on cost; response facilities can be built in; the message can be easily retained and re-examined any number of times.

Because television is a largely indiscriminate medium, addressing mass audiences, its use to bolster a direct mail sales campaign will only appeal normally to a large organization with a mass market. Which is not to say that direct mail is exclusively, or even primarily, a medium for that kind of situation. Indeed it can be a valuable partner in small local sales activities as well as in large national ones.

Take by way of example a marketing operation selling by traditional retail methods – through one corner shop, or a national multiple chain, it doesn't matter. The retail trade has traditionally regarded direct mail (and direct response, or off-the-page, advertising) in those areas (such as bookselling) where it is aware of its existence, as the enemy, competing – by methods frequently categorized as "unfair" – for a share of a fixed-size cake. Personally I have always regarded this as an unattractive, and usually erroneous, view of almost any market: the more people are persuaded, by whatever means, to buy books (or shoes, or computers, or jam doughnuts) the larger the market for books (or shoes, computers, or jam doughnuts) will become, to the benefit of *all* those selling these things. (I am reminded of the 1951 estimate by Remington Rand that the world-wide market for general-purpose digital computers was 27.) The experience, quoted above, of Reader's Digest discovering, albeit accidentally, that direct mail sales effort enhanced the sale of its books in bookshops, is striking evidence of this simple truth. But if direct mail and retail can reinforce each other by accident, they can achieve a great deal more when integration is planned and deliberate. Again, the possibilities for integration can best be seen by examining some of the principal strengths and weaknesses of each medium, and considering how they can best complement each other:

a) The weakness of the retail trade is that it is, in relation to its customers, an essentially *passive* medium. That is to say, the *customer* decides to "go shopping"; he makes the trip to the High Street, surveys the stores, decides which one to enter, and views selectively the goods on display. (Nowadays the goods probably have to be picked off the shelf and carried to a check-out counter as well.)

b) Direct mail, by contrast, is an *active* medium: the *seller* determines which prospects to approach, when, and in what numbers, in their own homes or offices. It is the seller who determines which product(s) to offer to whom, and which aspects of those products to highlight.

c) As against this, direct mail has two major weaknesses. First, the customer buying by mail must decide to order, and sometimes pay, in whole or in part, before seeing the goods. In some cases this doesn't greatly matter – for example where the product is fairly low-priced, so that "shopping around" for a bargain, or a slightly superior brand, is not a high priority for the consumer. The same may be true where the product is in some respect demonstrably unique: books, for example, or records, are not (except, perhaps, from Mills and Boon) interchangeable one with another. For that matter, uniqueness may lie in a very clear price advantage, as in the case of off-the-page offers of luggage, cutlery, cooking utensils. But in the case of high-priced consumer durables, the consumer's desire to see, touch, try out before making a commitment is likely to be paramount. It is to answer that desire that direct mail so often offers goods "on approval" or alternatively with money-back guarantees. But the consumer knows as well as the seller that to order on approval is more than half way to buying, and may remain reluctant.

Second, direct mail is widely distrusted – much less so than ten years ago, but still significantly. This is in part because direct mail transactions do not take place face-to-face between two people, but impersonally. This makes it difficult to cater for unique individual circumstances, to answer particular questions, to provide reassurance, and so on.

d) The retail trade is well-placed to overcome these problems. It offers premises where samples of the goods on offer – and frequently of other similar, competing goods – can be seen and evaluated. And it provides staff who, at least in theory, are equipped to answer questions, deal with customers' problems, and provide a human context for the sales transaction. (Argos is one example of a mixed-media sales operation distinct from the conventional retail pattern.)

So, how can these strengths and weaknesses be combined to produce a selling effort that makes the most of both worlds? One answer is to use direct mail as the initial approach to potential customers, with retail premises as the back-up where the sale is consummated. On this basis, a direct mail shot can be used to tell people of the existence of the shop (in particular where new premises are being opened) and its range of products, to advise them of a particular product, or a special offer, or to advertise a sales promotion scheme run by the shop. In this context the direct mail shot itself is not selling; it is being used as an advertising medium, supplying information – but with a very specific purpose directly related to the selling function. It is the purpose of such a direct mail piece to attract people to the shop concerned, at a time chosen by the seller, and in pursuit of objectives suggested by the seller. Used in this way, direct mail becomes an arm by which the retailer reaches out to the public, makes, and retains, contact with them. Direct mail becomes the retailer's second, mobile, shop window, with a potential audience many times larger, and more attentive, than the actual shop window.

But although the use of direct mail in ways of this kind is growing, it takes a while to wean people to new ways. Much more common than this form of integrated marketing (which is still the wave of the future) is the use of a direct mail offer as a straightforward selling medium. And in this connection the question one most often meets from marketers who have not used direct mail before is: how do I determine whether my product is suitable for sale by direct mail – what are the characteristics of a direct mail product?

## 2.1 Selling Consumables

It is astonishing, in all that has been written on direct mail and how to do it, in all the seminars and workshops that are held every year, that little or no attention has been devoted to this question. Perhaps this is because it doesn't seem like an easy one to answer: after all, London Bridge was, I am assured, sold by direct mail (although no doubt some form of conveyance other than the postal service was used for its actual delivery) so what does that exclude? Nevertheless, if we leave out extreme, or one-off, examples of this kind, it is possible, with a little thought, to lay down some useful rules of thumb. Like any other rules in business, they are valid only until someone finds a sensible way of circumventing them.

By far the most desirable characteristic of any product from the seller's point of view – and regardless of the medium through which it is to be sold – is that it should be, in some sense, consumable. Prime examples of the consumable goods traded through the mail are those offered by the mail order catalogue houses (Littlewoods, Freemans, J.D.Williams, GUS) being clothing, soft furnishings, and the like. Even more quickly consumable is a periodical, and although, in contrast to the USA, the UK sells the bulk of its periodical journals from news-stands, there are still some notable exponents among them of direct mail expertise. (Reader's Digest, Consumers' Association, Automobile Association.)

Books are one of the staples of the direct mail industry, as, to a lesser extent, are records. Books are an interesting case: their *contents* may be said to be consumable: reference books date, and have to be replaced, while most other books are read not more than once by any one person. Moreover, the medium-term consequence of buying, and reading, a book is probably to stimulate the appetite for books rather than to satisfy it. But the artefact itself tends not to be consumable: books, unlike magazines, are not thrown away, but gradually collect on shelves.

## 2.2  Selling Collectibles
For the key fact about books is that, while they are in one aspect consumable, they are in another aspect collectible – and if your direct mail product cannot have the one characteristic, then it is a useful second-best if it has the other. After all, the greatest cost in any form of marketing lies in locating your customers. What better then, having located them, than to have them spend the rest of their lives reordering the same consumable product, or alternatively, slightly different, collectible, versions of the same product.

The market in collectibles is a large one. The Post Office has carved out a lucrative slice with its commemorative stamps. This slice is worth some attention, because it illustrates a major dilemma inherent in this kind of market. A collectible owes some of its fascination for the collector to its scarcity – or better still its uniqueness. (In this sense London Bridge fits into our pattern after all: it was bought as a unique collectible.) Tied to this also is the expectation of a rising real value, which in turn is a result of demand exceeding supply – i.e. effective scarcity. Producers of collectibles, then, who saturate their market are undermining their own future position since, once they have met total demand there can be little prospect of values rising. In the case of the philatelic market, this is so large, and so international that the number of stamps of a given issue sold by the Post Office is not a serious problem – though the period of issue is still restricted. What does cause concern is how many new issues a given postal administration puts out in a year. The philatelic world keeps a close watch on this, and postal administrations which become greedy quickly find themselves blacklisted.

Producers of other collectibles do not usually have this kind of externally-imposed discipline, and many of them find the exercise of self-discipline rather demanding. So we live in a world, as it sometimes seems, rapidly silting up with commemorative medals, Royal wedding mugs, silver ingots engraved with vintage cars, and such-like bric-a-brac. The idea being, as with the book club, to transform a single transaction for the sale of one product into a continuing relationship where the once-captured goose goes on laying golden eggs for ever and ever.

One form of added incentive deployed by direct marketers in the collectible field is the concept of the "limited edition". This description is intended to stimulate the prospect's acquisitive instincts by implying that the product concerned will quickly gain scarcity value. The British Code of Advertising Practice – that arbiter of what claims are, and are not, acceptable in advertising copy – has attempted to curb the more blatant excesses of the "limited edition" school by insisting that the term must be accompanied by some form of qualification. The results to date have not always been enlightening – as one can see in the case of the "collectible" plates, whose editions are "limited" to, for example, "100 firing days" – whatever that may be thought to mean.

In sum then, it is highly desirable to have a product that is consumable, the craving for which is renewed automatically at regular intervals. Failing that, find something that is collectible; if it can also be fairly represented as likely to gain in value, that is a bonus. Not an easy recipe. But failure to observe it means a lot of hard work, and perhaps ultimate failure. Direct marketing in the seventies – particularly through the burgeoning colour supplements – took off into a whole new realm of watches, luggage, clocks, radios, clock-radios, cassette-radios, cassette-clock-radios ... items neither consumable, nor, normally, collectible. Many of these were very good value for money. Indeed the whole phenomenon (led in particular by one firm, Scotcade) did much to redeem the previously rather sleazy image of direct marketing. And in doing so sowed the seeds of its own destruction: if you sell Mrs Jones a six-piece suite of luggage, then the better it is, and the more she likes it, the less likely you are to sell her a second one. So you will have to find something else for encores. And then something else. And then...

## 2.3 Selling One-Offs

What then can we say about "one-off" items for sale by direct mail? Other than urging that you have an inexhaustible fund of new ideas? Well, there are some simple points of economics with which to start. First, do not pay too much attention to all that direct mail propaganda about how goods sold direct to the public are better value for money because they cut out the middle man. The economics of direct selling are different from those of retail selling – and not necessarily more favourable at all. What they do demand is a very healthy mark-up – something like three times. That is, if you have a product you are buying-in, or manufacturing, for £4, you are going to have to sell it for not significantly less than £12. (As the absolute sum of money increases, the required percentage mark-up will lessen somewhat – say to 2½ times.) Consider an illustration:

Product x is bought in at £4, and offered to an audience of 100,000 people by direct mail at £12. The resultant response rate, in terms of orders, is 5%. Then:

|  | £ |
|---|---|
| Cost of 100,000 pieces @ £300/thou. | 30,000 |
| Cost of 5,000 products @ £4 | 20,000 |
| Reply postage on 5,000 orders @ 15p | 750 |
| Handling 5,000 orders @, say, 50p | 2,500 |
| Despatching 5,000 products @ 75p | 3,750 |
|  | 57,000 |
| Revenue from 5,000 orders | 60,000 |
| Contribution to o'heads & profit | 3,000 |

Bearing in mind that this calculation makes no allowance for bad debts, returned products, etc., this is clearly not a recipe for getting rich quickly. If the prospect list is very good, and pulls 10% rather than 5%, things are, of course, better. Promotion cost doesn't change; other costs double, making a total cost of £84,800. Revenue doubles to £120,000, leaving a more sensible contribution of £36,000. But not that many direct mail promotions can be confident of pulling a response of 10% from a list of any size.

Again, promotion material need not cost £300/thousand. But with postage alone varying from £105 to £150 per thousand (depending on the rate of discount available) it isn't easy to get large reductions without reducing the impact of the promotion, and hence the response rate.

What we can deduce from examples of this kind is that, over and above the requirement for a three times mark-up, it is unlikely that a one-off product can be profitably sold by direct mail at a price significantly less than £15. (Unless, of course, you are prepared to pay a premium to build a list – or a database – of customers for future products.)

The ideal direct mail product, selling at £15 or more, and with a three times mark-up, will also be a unique product, or have important unique features, or be part of a unique proposition. If this is not so – if the product is simply a slightly different version competing with many others of essentially like kind – then the prospect will be less likely to buy it sight unseen. The seller, in fact, must produce a compelling reason why the prospect should do something so un-natural as to order an item sight unseen – and this can most easily be done by convincing buyers that *only* by doing so can they obtain such-and-such a unique benefit.

## 2.4 Distribution

Finally, consideration must be given to how the product, once sold, is to be conveyed to the purchaser. Distribution is an area where retail stands at a distinct advantage to direct mail. The manufacturer or wholesaler who requires to distribute in bulk to a limited number of retail outlets has an altogether more manageable problem than the direct mail seller, who must deliver single items to single addresses anywhere in the country. Retail shops that will deliver to consumers' homes are nowadays a rarity: such service is confined to bulky (and expensive) items. For the most part, the retail trade has solved its distribution problem by ignoring it; the customer is now aided by a private motor car, the shopkeeper's distribution agent. Direct mail has no such assistance. Most practitioners, already heavily involved with the postal service for the distribution of promotion material, turn naturally in the same direction for product distribution. This means that thought has to be given – from the inception of the campaign – to postal distribution costs, security of packaging, and such-like matters. Clearly a direct mail product will benefit by having a low weight-to-price ratio; at the extreme end of the spectrum, items which are too bulky for transmission by post carry a built-in disadvantage, unless a suitable national distributor can be found.

## 3  Market Research

This is the function in which direct mail differs most radically from other marketing media. Every marketing person preparing to launch a new product, or contemplating an attack, with an established pro-duct, on a new market, faces essentially the same problem: how to determine the size of demand for the product. Worse still, since demand is presumably a variable affected by other factors, such as price, credit terms, guarantee, etc., how to fix upon the optimum combination of variables that will produce the greatest profit.

The truth probably is that very few products or services are in fact sold on anything like optimal (from the seller's point of view) terms. If the product is being sold through traditional retail outlets, there are really three avenues to explore in trying to fix on the best set of terms for an offer. These are:

a) Discover what the competition is doing, and then decide whether to:
    i) undercut them, and risk a messy price war;
or ii) stress the improved features of one's own product.

or b) Establish a unit cost for whatever number of products:
    i) the sales manager says he can sell over a given period;
or ii) the warehouse has space for and add a percentage to cover selling costs, overheads, perhaps (if you think the market can stand it) profit.

or c) Commission a market research survey.

This last option has the advantage of getting the problem off the marketing manager's back for a few weeks, and into the hands of "experts" who can be relied upon to produce an impressive-looking report for the Board, suitably dressed up in Adspeak, and who can conveniently be blamed if anything goes wrong afterwards.

By contrast, market research in a direct mail context is not a separate area of endeavour employing different techniques from those familiar to the marketing department. The direct mail marketing manager doesn't rely on what people *say* they will do in a set of interviews, or on learned analyses of gaps in the market and disquisitions on "positioning". Market research in direct mail consists in actually selling your product to a sample of your intended audience in order to see how many takers there are on a given set of terms – or to several samples, varying the terms for each. And the conclusions derived from this are based upon what real people actually *do* in real circumstances – not on what they say they will, or might, do in quite different circumstances. Direct mail practitioners, in fact, don't talk about market research at all, in the sense of a separate set of techniques for assessing demand. They do talk, all the time, about testing – trying out this or that variation of price, premium, copy, colour, on sample segments of the market, measuring the response, and drawing conclusions.

That testing has its expertise is undeniable. But it is a mathematical, or statistical expertise, based upon actual occurrences in the real world. It will tell you:

"If, out of a representative sample of your audience, x% behave in a given way, then you can be 95% confident that, in identical circumstances, x, plus or minus y, % of your total audience will behave in the same way."

This still begs a few questions. What does 95% confidence mean? It means that the mathematics holds good 95 times out of every 100. Oh yes? And what about the other five times? Well, they're there to remind you that there is no such thing as certainty about a future event, and to keep you on your toes. And what does "identical circumstances" mean: after all, if I do a test mailing now and then mail my total audience in a month's time, the one thing I do know for certain is that the external circumstances won't be identical. Very true.

Nevertheless, the insights given by testing in a real market, instead of asking hypothetical questions, are real and worthwhile. This is not the place in which to describe the techniques of testing: the interested reader can find a full description elsewhere.* Suffice it to say that, whereas conventional market research techniques enable marketers at best to make a slightly more educated guess at the answers to their questions, direct mail testing enables direct mail marketers to calculate. The calculations are not infallible, and do not guarantee success every time. But those that use them will come out on the right side over a period.

Testing, of course, is not only about sounding out the market for a new product. One of the major differences between direct mail and the other marketing media is that in other media each sale tends to be a one-off event; in direct marketing each sale – indeed each promotion – creates a packet of information about the prospect, which is fed back to the promoter's records for future use. (It is this feedback that marks the distinction between a mere passive list of prospects and a dynamic database, as we shall see later.) Therefore, the object of each promotion sent out should be to generate as much information as possible, subject, of course, to cost constraints. When we research the market for a new product, we are testing a particular product/offer against break-even – will it be profitable or not? When we do a mailing for an established product, we should be taking the

---

* E.g. in a chapter by the present author entitled "Testing & Measurement" in the Direct Mail Handbook, 2nd ed. pub. by Exley, 1989.

opportunity to ask further questions – by comparative testing of one piece of copy against another, or of an attractive premium versus a price reduction. Testing is a continuous process of refining the terms of one's approach to the public by observing results and trying new methods.

There are people around who find this an unnecessarily energetic approach: for them the object of testing is to find the winning formula which they will then stick to come hell or high water. This is inadvisable. The universal law of entropy – which predicts that in time everything runs down – applies to direct mail as well as to astro-physics. Lists decay, response rates deteriorate. To combat this inexorable trend we must be continually looking for new approaches – and testing is the tool by which we can find a new formula before the old one becomes too tired to work.

## 4  Summary

To summarize, then, an initial approach to the use of direct mail should be characterized by the following steps:

a) Determine overall marketing objectives.

b) Devise a strategy for the use of advertising, selling, and market research resources to meet these objectives, with consideration of all available media.

c) Determine the functions required of the direct mail medium in relation to this strategy, taking into account the nature of the product/service being promoted, and the relative strengths and weaknesses of the medium in these circumstances.

d) Map out a series of activities through which the direct mail medium can carry out these functions.

e) Decide on the precise objective of each proposed activity.

f) Analyse the economics of each activity, and create a budget for it.

g) Select the appropriate audience for each activity.

h) Produce the necessary direct mail material, including appropriate response media, for each activity, and undertake the necessary mailings.

i) Handle response in line with undertakings in promotion.

j) Monitor response and analyse the actual economics of each mailing; compare with budget, and use these findings to modify, if necessary, further parts of the programme.

k) Ensure that a full record is kept of individual responses, thus modifying the nature of the potential audience for further mailings – or indeed other marketing activities.

These processes can be illustrated diagramatically, on the page opposite. From this illustration it can be seen that the whole process contains two feedback mechanisms – a vital aspect of all direct mail activity. The first of these is the feedback of an economic assessment of the degree of success or failure achieved by each mailing. The second is the feedback of individual data about each respondent – and, by implication, about each non-respondent. It is this second factor which makes possible the construction of a dynamic marketing database, and it is towards consideration of this possibility that we will now turn.

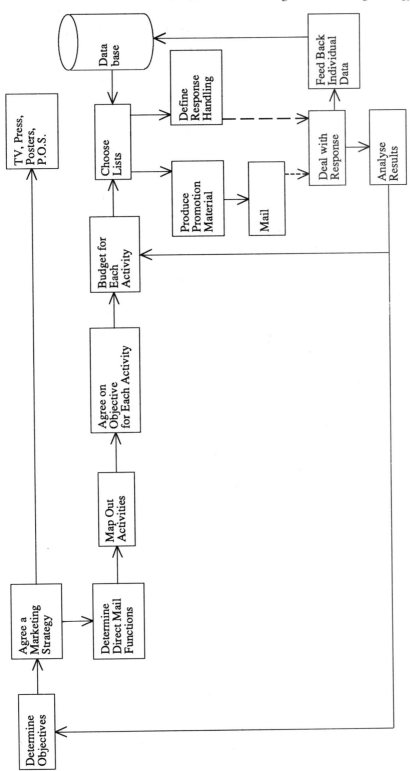

# 2 Database: The Concept

## 1 Definitions

The key to good direct mail has always been perceived as access to good prospect lists. Every seminar on direct mail has had something to say about lists – how to obtain them, how to use them, how to maintain them. Now suddenly the buzz-word is database; plain ordinary lists of names and addresses have been transformed overnight, and every direct marketing agency possessed of a microcomputer is offering database facilities to its bemused potential clients.

What is a database? The best answer might be: an exceedingly imprecise term. As frequently used, the term means nothing much more than a collection of information held on a computer and organized in some logical manner. (My old friend Drayton Bird defined it in a recent lecture as "...simply a list of people with relevant details about them placed on a computer".) On this definition, any old list of computerized names and addresses is a database. In this book we propose to use a more stringent set of criteria.

The term "database" was first coined at an American military seminar in 1963 on "Development and Management of a Computer-Centered Data Base". The same seminar produced the first attempt formally to define the term:

a) A database is a set of files.

b) A file is an ordered collection of entries.

c) An entry consists of a key, and data.

In other words, if a file is a collection of data entries, each of which can be accessed by a unique key, then a database is a set (i.e. a related collection) of such files. But this doesn't help much: in real life the question whether a given collection of data entries constitutes (or should constitute) a single file, or several different but related files, is no more than a matter of technical convenience. It would seem more useful to define a database with rather less reference to its conceptual structure, and rather more reference to its purpose, function, or potential. (Just as it may be more illuminating to define a knife as a hand-held implement for cutting things, rather than by reference to its shape, composition, size, colour, etc.) A database, then (at least for the purposes of this book) is:

a) a collection of data entries, which is

b) organized on a computer by

c) a software package, which

d) allows the user to relate, collate, summarize and reproduce such entries in accordance with any internally logical criteria.

If that sounds a frightful mouthful, let's try an example. A company is selling goods to consumers through 200 retail outlets. It is able to collect a certain amount of data about each retail transaction:

Customer name and address
Branch
Product purchased
Price
Method of payment
Date of purchase

This data, in relation to each sale, is held on a computer, which also holds further information about each customer:

Sex
Marital status
Credit limit
Current debt

and about each outlet:

Branch No.
Name of manager
City/suburban/town/rural
Current year's sales target
Sales year to date
Selling area in square feet

Now, there are several different ways in which this information can be structured in a computer (or in any other filing system). Theoretically, we could have a single file in which the individual data entries consisted of customer records, each keyed by a unique customer number, and each containing details of every transaction involving that customer, including full details of the outlet or branch at which the transaction took place. Such a file organization is perhaps unlikely, for two reasons:

a) There is a high degree of data redundancy: i.e. branch data is repeated many times, wasting storage space (which costs money) and probably costing much extra processing time as well.

b) It becomes a considerable exercise to extract branch-oriented information – e.g. to calculate the total sales for a given branch, one has to look at every sales transaction.

Alternatively, we could have a single file organized by branch rather than by customer. This reduces data redundancy (since there will be fewer purchases per customer than there are per branch) without eliminating it, since customer data will now have to be repeated for each branch purchase. Moreover, while it will now be simple to obtain information about a given branch's performance, it will be laborious to determine, for example, the total purchases of a single customer – who may, after all, patronize several branches.

One answer to these problems would be to have two files – one with data entries relating to customers and their transactions, and another with data entries pertaining to branches – but taking care to include in the branch file such extra items as:

Total no. of customer transactions in this branch
Total value of transactions in this branch

Each sales transaction would then affect both files; data redundancy would be at a minimum; branch statistics and customer profiles alike would be easy to derive.

However, it may be that in our imaginary company there is a frequent need for the production of product-based sales statistics – that we wish to discover, for instance, what proportion of product x sales, made through branch y, were paid for by Barclaycard. Such a need, or its possible prospect, might persuade the database designer to set up this application with three files:

Customer file (containing static data)
Branch file (as above)
Sales file (with one entry per sales transaction, keyed by product,
   and showing customer identification).

To which one might wish to add fourthly a product file, giving static details of each product, such as:

Source
Cost
Delivery lead-time

Now, the particular choice of method by which this data should be structured on the computer is a technical matter of little practical interest to the user – so long as the latter's needs have been properly identified and communicated in the first place. Moreover, the criteria for making such technical decisions themselves change over time, according to the relative cost of hardware and the relative sophistication and/or efficiency of software. What qualifies this collection of information to be called a database is not whether it is structured in one, two, or n files (which may well differ, on purely technical grounds, from one installation to another) but the fact that the computer software that controls the data is capable of data extraction, correlation, and summarization in pursuit of any logical demand. So, in this horribly over-simplified example, we would expect to be able to learn what proportion of purchases by married women had been paid for by Access, separately by branch; or to list all the male customers whose current debt was less than 25% of their credit limit, having made their last purchase more than three months previously.

   To call a collection of information devoid of this facility a database is about as meaningful as to refer to a tiger-skin rug as though it were the living animal: not only is the right software a necessary integral part of a database; it is actually the part that provides the nerves, muscles, brains, and sinews of the total organism.

   However, with the software as with the data itself, what matters is not what it looks like, or how or by whom it was constructed, but what it does. There is a tendency in some quarters to suppose that the term database can only be applied to a collection of data under the control of one or another piece of branded manufacturer's software listed as a Database Management System (DBMS for short). This is the opposite approach to that which would describe any old heap of information as a database – but it is equally a heresy. A variety of computer manufacturers have produced DBMSs for machines from micros to main frames, to provide general-purpose database facilities. Much of this software is expensive, both in itself and in its use of hardware – for the very reason that it is general-purpose. There is no reason in the world why special-purpose software cannot be written by users to support their own database applications, and there is no reason why an application running without a branded DBMS should not be at least as effective in meeting the needs of its user (and that is the criterion) as one supported by the latest IBM offering. On the contrary, a well-written special-purpose system will normally be much more effective, and much cheaper to run, (if one ignores the development cost) than its general-purpose cousin.

## 2  Database: Top-Down

We have seen, then, that a database is a collection of data entries with total inherent flexibility to meet the information needs of its users. But what users? What is the scope of the information covered, and what are the main uses to which, in a business context, it may be put? This book is primarily about marketing, and we will be concentrating in this chapter on database concepts as they are relevant to marketing needs. But it may be worthwhile to look first at the broader picture.

The earliest computer installations were each dedicated to performing a specific function. Thus, the first commercial computer installation in the USA (Univac I in 1951) was undertaken to process the results of the US census. In the UK, Leo I (also in 1951) was commissioned to calculate the daily provisioning of Lyons teashops. (A nice instance, I have always thought, of differing American and British priorities.) But the typical business application of these machines' successors throughout the 1950s and into the 1960s, was payroll – a well-defined operation which, if the scale was large enough, could always be performed more quickly and more cost-effectively on a computer than by previous methods. Payroll processing required access to tax tables and staff records; payment of various types of bonus might require reference to sales records at branches, or similar performance data. Files of information were built up; these could not be described as databases since they had little flexibility in use, or provision for data retrieval: they were not there to supply information on demand, but to perform a particular pedestrian and inflexible, unvarying, function.

In time the functions of the typical computer installation widened. The next candidate for computerization would probably be a series of accounting functions (partly because these too were relatively well-defined, partly because the financial director regarded the computer, originally dedicated to payroll, as part of his/her personal fiefdom, and its acolytes as his/her employees. The performance of accounting functions would require access to sales data, to branch records, to purchase orders – and, of course, to payroll data. Further files were created.

Later still stock control became a fashionable area for computerization as companies, in times of recession, attempted to rationalize their stock-holdings. This required a product file, stock records, a branch file, sales records, supplier records, records of purchase orders and deliveries.

And perhaps, at the end of it all, marketing had a shout: branch records, customer files, sales records, promotion records, salesmen's personnel records were required.

Somewhere along this line of development two things became noticeable:

a) Large areas of data redundancy were being opened up in the computer installation. (Of course, this data redundancy had always been implicit in the functional structuring of the company, but it had been neither so visible nor so noticeably expensive as it now became.) Thus, several different applications might require information about branch operations; if each application kept its own branch file, even where the information required might differ in detail between applications, a great deal of it would be common, and its repetition costly. Worse still, data redundancy leads inevitably to data inconsistency: the chances of a piece of data held in three different files being correctly maintained in all three over an extended period are small, and diminish over time.

b) On a more positive note, the enormous volumes of raw data being accumulated were capable, if only they could be collated, analysed, and reduced to manageable size, of providing new and valuable insights into the business.

The second of these considerations gave rise, in the 1970s, to the briefly-fashionable drive (which even found echoes in government policy at the time) towards "information systems" and "information technology". As is so often the case with business fashions (particularly when they are embraced by politicians) this produced a fair collection of disasters, and not too much is heard now of its erstwhile terminology. But from its ashes, with the added stimulus of the data redundancy/consistency problem referred to above, rose much of the thinking behind today's database concepts.

Unfortunately, not all of the lessons of earlier disasters have been learned – certainly not by the writers of textbooks. The first principle enunciated by theoretical works on database is that the process of data analysis and database design should be a "top-down" process: the analyst should look at *all* the information available to the organization, and at the totality of its needs – not at pre-defined functions or departments. As we shall see later, this counsel is more often than not impossible to follow in practice – and is frequently undesirable in the real world beyond the textbooks: it is a recipe for unmanageable mega-projects which consume large sums over long periods during which there is little or no visible result, with an almost total lack of accountability to any profit centre. But let us first see what is the rationale for this proposition, and where it is supposed, at least, to lead.

The idea is that the data analyst should begin by uncovering all of the data entities known to the organization: a customer, a branch, a product, a sales transaction, etc. To each entity he should attach all of its proper attributes:

| Entity: | Customer | Product | Branch |
|---|---|---|---|
| **Attributes:** | Ref. No. | Ref. No. | Ref. No. |
| | Name | Description | Manager's Name |
| | Address | Min. Order Qty | Address |
| | Sex | Cost | Location |
| | Marital Status | Lead Time | Sales Target |
| | Credit Limit | Min Stock | Selling Area |
| | Current Debt | Level etc. | etc. |
| | Total Purchases | | |
| | etc. | | |

Each entity, and each attribute, will appear once, and once only, in the analysis. Finally the analyst should describe the relationship between the listed entities:

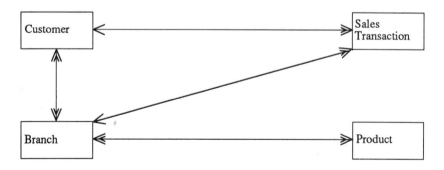

This diagram, being translated, tells us that a customer may patronize one or more branches (hence the two arrowheads pointing from customer to branch) and may have one or more sales transactions; a sales transaction can relate to one only customer, one only branch, and one only product; a product will have one or more sales transactions and be stocked at one or more branches; a branch will stock multiple products and serve multiple customers.

However, this is clearly a picture of a small part only of a company's operations. If we are truly operating on the "top-down" principle, then we must cover the totality, which might be shown thus:

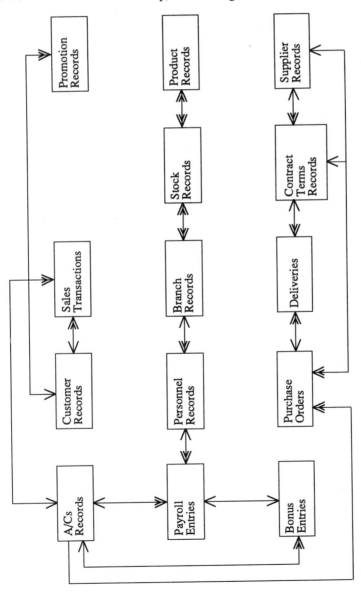

If, in our imaginary company, the first function to be computerized was payroll, followed by various accounting functions – sales ledger, purchase ledger, P&L etc – then, since all these functions are likely to fall within the single departmental orbit of the financial director, it is quite possible that by now the computer systems in which these functions are embedded have been so rationalized as to avoid *internal* data redundancy and inconsistency. It is also possible that the computer department may by now have escaped from the financial director's icy embrace, to become a *company* resource, headed, who knows, by a data processing director. (If this has not happened, then in all probability each of the other departments such as marketing, buying, personnel, stock control, will have acquired its own computer, and any further chance of rationalization on anything larger than a departmental scale will have totally vanished for the foreseeable future.)

What one may be fairly certain of, however, is that when the Personnel Department computerizes its functions, whether centrally or on its own equipment, it will not simply add data to the existing record of personnel used for payroll purposes: firstly, the payroll/accounting system is probably structured with insufficient flexibility to make this possible without stripping it down and starting again; secondly, such a process would raise questions regarding restrictions on data access, priority of access, and other points of inter-departmental protocol which there is no ready means within the company of resolving. So the Personnel Department will have its own personnel files, and the Accounts Department its own overlapping ones, and they will be in some degree inconsistent, which will, from time to time, drive the managing director into a rage – but not often enough to make him take decisive action. Similarly, we may be sure that the Marketing Department and the Buying Department will have overlapping branch records and product records. And, if the Marketing Department is already using customer records and sales records for selective direct mailing, these records will certainly overlap with, and probably in some particulars contradict, the sales ledger records within the accounting system. And so on.

Elementary logic suggests that a preferable, more efficient, scenario must be one in which there is a single, central, company data resource to which all users have access for that data which they require to perform their particular functions – a company-wide database which eliminates data redundancies and inconsistencies, and which allows total flexibility in analysis, collation, and recovery of data. But elementary logic can be wrong.

First, a "top-down" data analysis can only usefully be performed by, or at least under the close control of, someone who himself fully understands the total needs of the business and the inter-relationships of its various parts. In an ideal world the data processing director would be such a person. In addition to an understanding of the business, the director would have the ability to convince departmental colleagues of the need for a central database approach, of the advantages each stood to gain, and of the qualifications of the team of analysts to referee tricky inter-departmental problems of access and priority. Alas, we don't live in an ideal world, and there are few data processing directors capable of such a role. This is not at all what one might have expected twenty years ago. It did seem at that time that the computer industry was destined to provide a ladder of advancement for its brighter staff analogous to the ladder climbed with such agility by accountants in a previous generation. It hasn't worked that way. While any number of men and women have now emerged from the chrysalis of the accountancy profession as fully capable heads of great companies, data processing personnel have rarely been able to achieve this transformation. The typical data processing manager, or director, today is departmentally-oriented rather than company-oriented – more interested in (or worried by) the problems of hardware capacity and software performance than in user requirements, which on the whole appear to be an imposition, and burdened by a serious communication problem with colleagues, which arises from being so thoroughly immersed in computer-speak as almost to have lost the use of the English language. Like most successful revolutionaries, having scaled the walls of the citadel, such a director/manager is now busy pulling up the ladder to cries of "I'm all right, Jack". He/she has no desire to lead a further revolution in thinking and in practice (which is what a company database is) but only wishes to protect what is already there.

Secondly, the computer department in any large company is loaded already well beyond the point at which it can contemplate a major new project. In my first job as a computer manager, we had a staff of two analysts and six programmers. In ten months we created a marketing database with two million customer records; management insisted that in the computer purchase proposal we include a paragraph on how we would dispose of this substantial staff, which would clearly not be required in such numbers, once the computer system was working to specification. Ten years later, we had a systems staff of 30, and a six months' lead time on the start of any substantial new project. Quite simply, the task of maintaining computer systems once written is much greater than is ever allowed for, even by the "experts". So capacity to handle new projects scarcely ever exists in "mature" computer installations.

Theoretically there are three ways of dealing with this bottleneck.

One can recruit a new team to handle the new project. The trouble is that the state of the labour market in computer staff is – and for twenty years has been – such that a single company's chances of picking up the four or five highly qualified staff required to build a company database are nil. Or, one can take drastic measures to *make* space in the existing schedule. This will mean axing a number of projects that have already spent several months in the pipeline waiting their turn, and freezing existing systems for all but the most unavoidable changes (e.g. those necessitated by legislation). Neither of these measures will make the Data Processing Department, or the database project, popular with the users of existing systems, or the promoters of other new projects. More importantly, such a decision involves a substantial hidden cost – the cost of not doing a number of things one would otherwise do. Or, one can use outside assistance. And it is to those who have a need of such assistance, whether in building a database or mounting a direct marketing campaign, that this book is largely directed. So we will return to this subject later on.

The third snag in the way of developing a comprehensive, company-wide database is that such a project means not just freezing the development of existing systems, but actually changing them. The financial director with a smoothly-functioning sales ledger system doesn't want *his/her* file subsumed in some corner of a huge company database; still less does he/she want months of picking out bugs in the new system, re-training staff, etc. (He/she can still remember the last time.) And the same goes for all his/her colleagues with functioning systems. Nor are these objections purely chauvinist (though they are that too). The cost to a company of a major systems upheaval running across several departments is likely to be extremely high, even if all goes more smoothly than the norm. And if things go just rather badly, it can be catastrophic.

Finally, creation of a company-wide database is a very lengthy process. Of course, the actual construction of the database can, if done carefully, proceed in a modular fashion, with each function converting to its use one at a time, and each in turn gaining from its introduction without having to wait for the total structure to be complete. But the data analysis and database design which must precede construction cannot be modular – and these will occupy, necessarily, 70-80% of the total elapsed time anyway.

Bearing these considerations in mind, it is perhaps scarcely surprising that company-wide databases, much talked about in the textbooks, are a bit thin on the ground. (To tell the truth I don't know of any.) Rather, what one is accustomed to find is the function-oriented database, filling the needs of one function, or perhaps one department. Of these partial databases, the most common is the marketing database. And since this book is essentially about various aspects of marketing, this is the type of database we will now consider at greater length. Its visual representation at a conceptual level might look something like this:

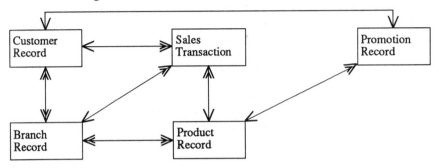

And its relationship to the oranisational structure of the company, like this:

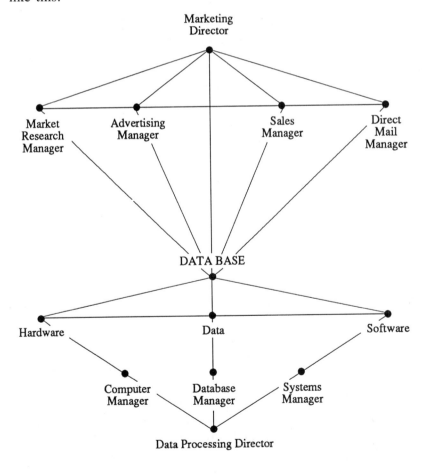

### 3  Database: Know Your Customer

At the heart of database marketing lies the collection of information about customers and prospects, their characteristics, tastes, habits, and life styles. For marketers who have a long-standing involvement with direct mail, such collecting has long been an important part of life – since, indeed, well before modern database techniques became available to help with the flexible use of such information. For many others, lacking the direct mail addict's necessity to think of customers as individual entities each living behind a separate letterbox, the penny has been extraordinarily slow to drop. Over every marketing director's door should appear, in letters of fire, not the ancient Greek admonition to "Know Thyself" (perhaps few of us would altogether care to do that), but rather:

KNOW YOUR CUSTOMER

Know him, that is, not simply as a reader of the *Sunday Times* colour supplement, of whom, by virtue of his reading habits, certain characteristics can be predicted, in the sure knowledge that, wildly inaccurate though they will be for a high proportion of the individuals concerned, they are correct for a larger proportion than in the case of *News of the World* readers. Know him, not as a member of some artificial statistical entity from whose normative characteristics many members of that entity will in practice diverge widely; know him, rather, as an individual person, with a name, living in a house, employed in a job, buying certain products, pursuing certain interests.

It's a strange thought when you consider it: shopkeepers who run corner shops and number their customers in scores, or perhaps hundreds, know their customers in just this way. Direct mail marketers, who number their customers, in many cases, in millions, can at least be said to be trying. But in between are the big department stores, for example, who neither know nor attempt to discover anything at all about their customers – unless they are account customers, who, boringly, have to be billed. In the Good Old Days when I first had a bank account, my bank manager knew me as a person (rather better than most of my friends). Today I have accounts at two banks and two building societies; I haven't so much as met a branch manager from any of them, and they (or rather their systems) know nothing more of me than the bare requirements for keeping my accounts more or less arithmetically correct, and sending statements.

This has to be crazy. We are sometimes told that the UK has the world's most efficient retailing network. (This has been alleged, for example, as a major reason for the UK's high propensity to import foreign goods.) If true, this says something pretty awful about the retail trade in other countries, because in the UK it has scarcely yet begun to understand what marketing is about.

Retail shops, for the most part, are idle, unimaginative, and almost entirely passive institutions. They squat in the High Street waiting for anonymous customers to overcome their own natural inertia and walk in through the doors. They undertake a little, impersonal, local advertising to encourage store traffic – but for the most part expect manufacturers to create demand by national brand advertising. And when any customers, acting on their own initiative, venture inside their premises, they are, in an ever-increasing number of cases, expected to discover for themselves what is on sale, at what price, to serve themselves, to transport their own purchases to a cash desk, and, after queuing (a necessary British ritual on all occasions) to carry them thence to wherever they wish to go – a destination of no interest whatever to the store.

That this process should have gone furthest in food stores is scarcely surprising, since it is there that the phenomenon of the repeat customer can be most completely relied on, with minimal encouragement required from the store. People need to buy food regularly; there is little to choose in quality between the stocks of one multiple food retailer and another, nor a great deal in price. So repeat visits become a matter of convenience first, and then of habit. It is much more surprising that shops selling products that demand less frequent replacement should show so little – almost no – interest in securing repeat custom, or in increasing the frequency of repeat visits.

It isn't only in the matter of reinforcing customer loyalty and encouraging repeat visits that retail stores appear to be blind to the need to know who their customers are, individually. In getting new custom also, they are equally unimaginative. I bought a house recently in a reasonably prosperous part of North London, which is served by a department store that is part of the John Lewis empire. The house was marketed through an estate agent. It would not have been difficult, or unreasonable, for the estate agent to have advised the department store of completion, and for me to receive a promotion offering the store's services in relation to new curtains, carpets, light fittings, etc. No such thing occurred. If I want to buy new curtains, it is up to me to find where my local department store is, and to visit it in person. If I am *very* lucky a sales assistant will condescend to take an order from me – although of course I will not be allowed to obtain any actual goods costing more than a fiver in anything under six weeks.

The behaviour of our great financial institutions is even more extraordinary. Retail stores can (and do) excuse their own idleness by remarking that it is very difficult to collect names and addresses from their customers, and liable to cause resistance. (We will return to this point later.) But banks, building societies, insurance companies, finance houses, all require names and addresses – together with an immense amount of personal information – as a condition of doing business, and they at least encounter no measurable resistance to its collection. Yet David Ogilvie could still say:

"I have life insurance policies with three companies. None of these has ever written to me suggesting that I buy *more* insurance from them. Bloody fools."

Admittedly that was in 1965, and it is true that things are now, slowly, changing. One of the most powerful catalysts is the Big Bang of 1986, which is changing the nature of the marketing problem for financial institutions from that of selling a single range of services *ex*tensively to the population at large, to that of selling a much wider range of services *in*tensively to existing customers. And in order to sell with maximum effect to named persons, it follows that one should know as much as possible about each one, and should use that knowledge in determining what to offer to each, and how to persuade each prospect to buy.

It doesn't greatly matter what one is selling, or what marketing media are in use – the following rules apply:

Know *who* your customers are, individually, not just as statistical groups.
Know *what* each has bought from you, at *what cost*.
Know *when* each has bought, and *how often*.
Know as much as possible of *how* each lives, in terms of life style.

Those lecturers on direct mail who like to have their admonitions wrapped up in some easily memorable formula refer to this as the Recency, Frequency, Monetary formula. Personally, I find it easier to remember the admonitions than the formula – but each to his own taste.

Why is this so important? Basically there are two reasons. The first has always been true, and is no more than a matter of common sense: people buy more readily products they know from suppliers they know – provided they have had a reasonable experience the first time round. So, reactivating old or existing customers is always easier – i.e. more effective per unit of cost – than obtaining new ones. What may be less immediately obvious, but has also been repeatedly found to be true, is that even lapsed customers – for example those who cancel their subscriptions to a magazine, or a club, or a charity – can, at least in the aggregate, be persuaded back into the fold more readily than cold prospects.

Of course, it is much easier to make repeat sales if one is selling a consumable product which requires regular replacement, but the same criteria apply to cross-selling, where the problem is to turn purchasers of one product into buyers of a range of products: in both cases the more one knows about one's customers the greater one's ability to target a sales message to the right people at the right time, and the more cost-effective one's efforts.

The second reason why knowledge of this kind is important is of relatively recent, and still increasing, significance. The years after the last war saw, in every developed country, an explosion of pent-up demand for consumer goods (and indeed capital goods) that were in short supply. For many years it was possible to make a lot of money by selling relatively undifferentiated products to a hungry, not very discriminating, mass market. With the gradual satisfaction of the most obvious consumer wants, and the attainment of a much higher level of overall prosperity, the situation has changed radically. The days when Ford could promise their customers a car in any colour, so long as it was black, are gone for good; the market is no longer characterized by an excess of demand over supply. The mass market, in consequence, has for some years past been breaking down for product after product, into a whole series of sub-markets. A food-store today can't just stock instant coffee as an alternative to the real thing. It must stock coffee beans as well as ground coffee, both from a variety of different locales and in numerous varieties of strength and flavour; the ground coffee must also be in varieties suitable for several different methods of preparation. Instant coffee will be stocked in several different brands, decaffeinated or ordinary, and again in several varieties of taste, and price. Motor cars must be available as manual or automatic, petrol or diesel, differentiated by colour and trim, as well as the presence or absence of some twenty different accessories permed every which way. Even the nation's cats have got in on the act, so that their food is sold in a dozen different brands, each available in ten flavours and two sizes.

This fragmentation of markets is still continuing, in virtually every product area, and demands from the marketer a much deeper understanding than before of a much more knowledgeable, more choosy, and less extensive market.

# 3 Database Applications

The information contained within a database may be used for a wide variety of marketing purposes (bearing in mind that non-marketing purposes lie, on the whole, beyond the scope of this book). It may be useful to take two or three typical sets of circumstances, and see how database facilities might be used to further the needs of the organization in each case.

## 1 Retail

Having already described above, in very broad terms, some of the characteristics of a retail marketing database, we will start there. Let us suppose a company with a chain of 100 garden centres, selling plants, seeds, fertilizers, pesticides, implements – everything connected with gardening. These centres are spread through the southern half of England, mostly in suburban areas; individual purchases can range from a pound or two to two or three hundred pounds; centres range in size from small shops with an annual turnover barely reaching six figures to substantial nurseries which take that much in a good weekend.

This small chain is the result of rapid growth in the recent past: when it was a much smaller outfit, management had a fairly clear view of the dynamics of each centre – who shopped there, for what, and why; to what extent repeat visits could be looked for, and how frequently; what products were likely to do better in one centre than another, and so on. But with the rapid expansion, this instinctive "feel" for the market in each centre is no longer possible, and there is nothing much yet to replace it. Of course, when considering opening a new centre, management looks at the demographic structure of the surrounding area: are the houses old or new; are the gardens large or small, mature or not; are the inhabitants young, middle-aged, or elderly; is the soil acid or alkaline; what are the figures for rainfall and sunshine. All of this will condition a decision to open in an area or not, and/or what type of centre, dealing in what range of products, to set up. But after the decision is made, and the centre opened, there is very little feedback of hard quantified data about who uses it and how frequently. Certainly, a pattern of product demand will emerge: management will know how much potting compost is sold in one outlet rather than another, and so on. But about the people who buy the potting compost, or the Rotavators, there is no information, beyond the unquantified impressions of local staff, at all.

Moreover, medium term results at some of the newer centres have been disappointing. Centres set up within reach of well-to-do new housing estates have turned in splendid early results as the first occupiers of the new houses have laid down lawns and bought lawn-mowers, planted fruit trees and herbaceous borders, dug and mulched and sprayed. Naturally, it wasn't to be expected that the initial level of activity from such a source would continue indefinitely, but the fall-off has been greater than can be explained simply by the satisfaction of early need for heavy investment: it is almost as though interest in the whole pursuit of gardening has come to occupy a much lower place in local priorities.

Management has determined that it needs to know a great deal more about its customers. In the short-term it has employed some "snap-shot" surveys, using face-to-face market research conducted with its customers. Long-term, however, management is convinced that it must build a permanent customer database which will comprise all available information about its *individual* customers. The objectives which it is hoped the database, once in use, will achieve, are several:

a) By telling management who its customers are and where they live, it will make post-purchase communication possible. The purposes of such communication will be:

    i) to obtain direct customer feedback of satisfaction or dissatisfaction, and reasons for same;

    ii) to establish or enhance customer loyalty;

    iii) to encourage more frequent visits and thus increase turnover.

b) By examining which groups of customers respond most readily to such communications, it will be possible to target such approaches more precisely, improving their cost-effectiveness.

c) From close examination of customers' individual characteristics, buying habits, etc., it will be possible to form hypotheses about which products should most appropriately be offered to which persons, about the most suitable tone and emphasis of promotion, and so on. Moreover, such hypotheses can be tested, and refined, over time.

d) By analysing sales according to age, sex, frequency, value, etc., it will be possible to establish whether the "instinctive" criteria hitherto used for establishing new centres continue to make sense, or whether there are previously unrecognized factors at work in determining purchasing habits. In particular, it will be possible to build a demographic "model" of a centre's customers, to compare this with the demographic profile of the area that the centre serves, and to derive from this comparison new criteria for locating outlets. (For more on demographics, see Chapter 4, Section 2, below.)

e) Although a prime purpose in communicating with customers is to increase traffic in the centres, it may also be possible, for part of the product range at least, actually to sell by mail – more particularly where offers are going to those who have already experienced and approved the quality of the company's products.

f) Communication by mail can also be used to solicit and obtain additional information about customers, their families, their gardens, and the purposes for which they use them – information which many customers will gladly volunteer if they believe it will be used to help the company structure its product range and its advertising in a more relevant way.

g) By enabling management to identify frequent visitors and/or high spenders, the database opens the possibility of all sorts of added-value schemes – gardening clubs, discount cards, competitions, and shows.

The conceptual framework of a marketing database to pursue these objectives can be represented as shown already on p. 00. There will be a record for each customer, and a record for each sales transaction. Sales will be related to customers, and both customers and sales will be related to branches (i.e. individual centres). Promotion transactions will also be recorded, indicating the promotions sent to particular customers. Sales and promotions relate to records of products, and product records in turn relate to individual centres, so that product movement can be analysed either overall, or by individual centre – or indeed in relation to customers living in a certain type of area and incurring expenditure in a given range over a specific six-month period (for instance).

It is, of course, a pity that the company, having been in operation for a number of years already, has irretrievably lost all the customer-related information that passed through its hands in that time. (As one might expect, much of the product-related information has been retained.) But that is water under the bridge; the vital thing now is to staunch the continuing haemorrhage of information. This brings us to a problem that confronts all would-be builders of databases – a problem that is, however, particularly acute in a retail environment – how does one collect customer data for one's database in the first place?

Clearly, data relating to branches, to products, and indeed to promotions, is totally within the company's control, and can be retained and formatted in any required way. The data that the company has never retained in the past is that relating to customers, and to sales at an individual transaction level. Each sale is rung up at a till, which produces a receipt for the customer, and records the product bought, and the payment, for accounting and stock analysis purposes. This, in future, will not be enough. The minimum information required now in respect of each sale is:

Customer name and address
Date
Branch
Product
Price
Method of payment

Of these items, by far the most troublesome is the first – the customer's name and address. The difficulty has two sources: the customer, who may be unwilling to provide the data, and/or irritated at being asked, and the assistant, who regards this as an unnecessary and time-consuming chore at the best of times, and, in busy times, as an imposition getting in the way of the real job of serving customers and keeping queues to a minimum.

Different circumstances will suggest different ways of coping with customer reluctance. Customer credit accounts, or store discount cards dispose of the problem for those purchases where they are used. Normally it makes sense to ignore customer data in respect of purchases below a given minimum amount. Customers paying by cheque can usually be persuaded to write their address on the back (their name being already pre-printed on the front). Filling in a product guarantee card for the customer can be another way of acquiring the desired information. Anything that has to be delivered produces the data automatically. A promise of a full refund within 28 days for any product returned together with an invoice bearing full customer details, may also do the trick.

Staff reluctance is another matter. Sometimes it amounts to little more than laziness; often it springs from a feeling that there is no immediate benefit the assistant can see from this chore to offset the disadvantage of keeping customers waiting, and perhaps irritating them as well. A staff incentive scheme may help – where staff are rewarded with a bonus on a sliding scale according to the proportion of sales where a full name and address is captured. Even more important is a training programme which will show branch staff what the database can achieve *for their branch,* and why it is therefore vital to keep it supplied with accurate information.

In the case of our illustrative garden centre company, each centre will be equipped with an electronic till incorporating a microcomputer. "Regular" customers will have discount cards and/or credit accounts – and their names and addresses will be stored permanently in the micro. Other customers, buying goods worth £15 or more, will be given a refund guarantee which holds good on the production of a full sales invoice, and will be asked to give names and addresses for this purpose. Staff at each branch will attend a full two-day residential course on database, as it affects branch dealings with customers, and there will be a bonus scheme for all branch employees, based on monthly success in improving store takings over the previous year.

## 2  Wholesale

Consider the case now of the wholesaler (or manufacturer for that matter) selling to business outlets. Interestingly, this user's database does not look very different in outline from that which we have been examining in the retail case below:

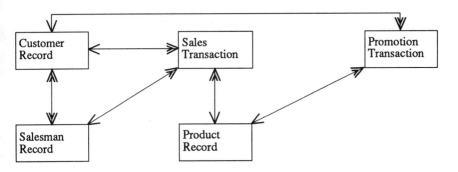

In this instance the salesman has replaced the branch; since a sales-man, unlike a branch, doesn't stock products, there is no relationship expressed between salesman's record and product record; otherwise the relationships are unchanged.

For our hypothetical case this time let us take a chemical company selling industrial cleaning materials to hotels, hospitals, schools, and other such large institutions. The materials are, over a large part of the range, consumable, and therefore require fairly frequent re-order-ing. The client does not wish to attempt a mechanical re-ordering system: there is strong competition in the field, and he feels com-pelled to maintain a personalized customer contact through a team of salesmen who are trained to provide an advice service in all manner of cleaning problems, as well as to cross-sell further products to customers who take less than the whole range.

Each of the company's salesmen has, on average, 80 active cus-tomers within a territory; each salesman also has a further 200 pros-pects, each of them using one or more products from a rival manu-facturer to which there is a valid alternative. The sales force has a higher turnover of staff than it should have; training is not very good and customer knowledge rather poor; morale is low.

Although the outline of available data and its relationships is little different from the retail case, the purposes for which management wishes to use a database are rather different:

a) By analysis of individual customer orders, service calls, usage rates, etc., to be able to provide an information and advisory service to the salesmen, enabling them to schedule their calls on existing customers more productively.

b) By maintaining a register of prospects, with all available details, to provide a similar prospect service to the salesmen.

c) To be able to retain all available customer and prospect information within the company, regardless of the comings and goings of individual salesmen.

d) To target relevant promotion material to customers and prospects by mail in a manner and time-scale programmed to enhance the activities of the salesmen.

In order to build and maintain a database that will fulfil these purposes, the following information will be required for each sales call made by each salesman:

Name and address of organization called on
Contact name and position
Date of call
Product code & quantity of each item ordered
Servicing functions performed
Index of customer satisfaction
Principal competitors

In this type of application there is little or no problem in acquiring information from the customer; the problem lies in motivating the salesmen, who have an in-built dislike of paper-work, head offices, routine, directives, computers, and so on. A number of companies have in the past tried to use computer systems to dictate to their salesmen their daily, weekly, or monthly, pattern of calls – often with poor results. Salesmen are by definition loners, and highly individualistic; let them suppose they are being scheduled by a machine and most of them will start to treat the computer as an enemy, ignoring its schedules, and failing to feed back the information it requires. What is therefore essential is to convince the salesman that the computer is acting as an assistant, not a would-be master. To this end, in our above example, the computer's first function will be to provide, from its database, a printed memorandum regarding the affairs of each customer or prospect on its *suggested* list of forthcoming calls. The information on this memorandum will include:

Name and address of organization
Name(s) and position(s) of contact(s)
Date each contact last visited
Products currently in use

Date & quality of last order for each product
Average usage rate for each consumable product
Other products deemed relevant to this customer
Chief competitors
Promotion material sent since last visit, with date(s)
Any responses received to above
Servicing problems over last six months
Index of customer satisfaction on last call

Of course, the salesmen can ignore the computer's recommendations on calling (and anyway, the computer can't take account of emergency servicing calls that the salesmen may receive to disrupt their schedules). But once they find the computer is working with them, not against them, attitudes will change; if the computer is the only source of information that can help them sell, and if that information is most readily available on accounts/prospects selected by the computer, then they will learn to co-operate.

When a company like this has a sales force that trusts its computer database, there is a further possible stage. One can give the salesmen terminals, at their office bases or homes, on which they can interrogate the database, and view customer or prospect data on their screens. One large pharmaceutical company already does this with its sales force of over 400 salesmen, who are able not merely to access customer data remotely, but also to initiate such actions as delivery of samples, or of printed promotion material, by post. Or, again, one can give the salesmen portable terminals and modems which they can take by car to their customers' premises, plug in and interrogate the database in front of the customer – an impressive demonstration of technical expertise.

For a lot of companies that have traditionally employed salesmen, a prime question must nowadays be whether this is still the most cost-effective way of selling, given the changing cost structures of recent years. There is no real point in trying to deal with this question in general terms – beyond pointing out that, of all the marketing media available, direct mail has had the lowest cost escalation over the last ten years, or any part of that period. Direct mail is not, however, an adequate *sales* instrument for all occasions or all products. What it can do, as in the case illustrated here, is to provide invaluable backing to render the time of the prime (and expensive) sales instrument – the salesman – more cost-effective. And it can do this through the discriminating power of a good database, which can be used selectively to mail customers and prospects, to analyse their responses, and to determine which are most likely at any given time to repay a salesman's effort in calling.

## 3 Direct Mail Selling

So far we have looked at one example where the function of the database, operating through direct mail promotions, is to bring more trade into retail shops; and at another example where the database exists to facilitate analysis of customer information so as to assist the efforts of the sales force, and also, via direct mail promotions, to determine which prospects are most worth calling on. In both instances direct mail plays a subsidiary role in the actual selling function, while being an integral part of the overall marketing scheme. We will consider now the function of the database in the classic direct mail operation where postal communication is the sole link between seller and buyer, and where direct mail is not merely a medium for advertising and/or for market research, but also for selling.

Let us take as our example a company that has for some years past been selling, by direct mail, books, prints, video tapes, records – a whole range, in fact, of leisure material. The company's first introduction to the direct mail market was by way of renting other peoples' lists, and sending its promotion material to those names. Early on the question arose whether it was best to aim one's promotion for a given product at a list of people who had bought some analogous product from someone else – e.g. to promote records to a list of guarantee-card holders on a range of record players – or at a list of people who had previously bought *by mail*, regardless of product. And early on the lesson was learned that, while there is never a 100 per cent answer to a generalized question of this kind, nevertheless time and again the factor of having previously bought by mail proves to be the most powerful single discriminator of those who are likely to purchase anything else at all by that medium.

This having been found to be the case, the conclusion was very quickly reached that the names of those who bought the company's products by mail would be the most valuable future asset of all – having the double bond of being mail purchasers and customers, for related products, of the company. So, from an early stage of operations, the names and addresses of orderers, which were already being passed through a computer system for the purpose of achieving despatch of goods, handling of accounts receivable, and so on, were retained so that they could be promoted later for other products.

This idea that one's own past customers were by far one's best future prospects was triumphantly vindicated, so that as the company's own list of buyers grew, so the need to rent outside lists diminished. But quite quickly a snag appeared. As the company's range of products increased, it wanted to offer new products to old customers, and old products to new customers. At first this wasn't too difficult: since each name and address was allocated a sequential customer number, it was possible to deduce how long a given customer had been on file, and the time for which each product had been on offer was also known. But, as time went on, the range of products widened, and the pattern of promotions became more complex. Shortly, it was impossible to tell with any certainty which individual customers had, at one time or another, been offered what products. And it became clear that the list of names and addresses had to carry information also about purchases and promotions, in order to avoid repetitiously offering the same product to persons who had either already bought it or who had indicated, by non-response to a promotion, a lack of interest in it.

So, what had started as a simple list of names and addresses of buyers, began to accumulate packages of more specific information. There was now recorded, for each customer sale:

Date of purchase
Product
Price
Method of payment
Speed of payment

And for each promotion sent out:

Date of promotion
Product
Offer
Response

Moreover, it was clearly convenient, as well as holding details of these individual transactions, to have a summary for each customer, showing:

Date of origin
Total no. of purchases
Total value of payments
Total promotions sent
Date of last order
Promotions since last order

The accumulation of this information not only made it possible to perform the relatively simple exclusions that had motivated this development, so that customers were not promoted for products they had already bought, etc. It also encouraged the marketing department to look again at the old question of product affinities. They had already proved to their own satisfaction that undiscriminated buyers-by-mail were better prospects than retail purchasers of related products – and that their own customers were the best prospects of all. But given that their own customers, now almost their total marketing universe, were all mail buyers in the first place, might it not also be true that segments of this universe might be better, or worse, prospects for a given product according to the nature of what they had bought before?

Unsurprisingly, this proved to be the case. In addition, other factors were found, by trial and error, to be significant too – speed of payment for example. So that quite quickly the company was faced with the need to select prospects for mailings on the basis of quite complex algorithms. The original programmes for handling the early name and address list had provided merely for its reproduction on labels. Simple options had been introduced to allow for printing out a 1 in n sample instead of the whole list, or to print only one or more geographically defined areas. Further modifications had made possible a certain amount of personalization, so that addresses could be printed at the head of letters, and appropriate salutations added. But a requirement to address all male customers who had purchased more than one product, including either product x or product y, but excluding those who had already bought product z, those who had received more than five promotions since their last order, and those who had not yet paid in full for their last purchase – this required a major programming effort, and this effort had to be repeated for each such new requirement.

What was required, and what was provided, was a general purpose piece of software that would accept any logical algorithm (or collection of logical algorithms) and produce the required results (counts, labels, or promotion letters) without further ado. And with the production of this piece of software (but not before) the company found itself with a functioning database.

For a while the facilities provided by this new software were more than enough to meet the demand for their use. But not for long. The desire for discriminatory information about individual customers grew as it fed. It wasn't enough to infer a customer's tastes, habits, income, life style from the limited number of products he or she bought from the company; rather the company wanted to have access to direct information on those and similar subjects. What kind of

Database Applications/57

house does the customer live in? What sort of car does he or she drive? How many children does he or she have, and in what age range? Has he or she a garden?

How could such information – demographic and psychographic as it is customarily referred to – be obtained? Worse still, how could it be used? For the point had now been reached where the sheer volume of data becoming available on individual customers was too great for the construction of selection algorithms by mere common-sense methods. And the number of possible permutations of data made controlled testing of alternatives – if conducted on anything like a comprehensive basis – horrendously expensive. What was required was a set of techniques whereby the *computer* could be persuaded to construct the selection algorithms for itself – predicting, in effect, which groups of customers were the best prospects for which products. And by great good fortune a set of techniques, developed for a quite different purpose, but suited to this one, lay ready to hand. These techniques are most commonly referred to in the direct marketing industry under the generic label of regression analysis, and we will describe their use, as well as considering the source and application of demographic and psychographic data in a later chapter. (See Chapter 6 below.)

Despite the extended quantity of information made available by tapping sources other than the simple occurrence of a sale or a promotion, and despite the extra complexity involved in the use of regression analysis, the actual picture of a direct mail database such as we have been considering is extremely simple:

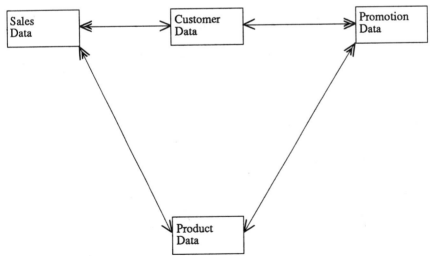

Where the file is a very large one, relative to the total population (i.e. running into millions) problems of data redundancy may suggest a slightly more complex arrangement, where the data common to all customers living in a given area is held once only in a record of that area, giving a picture like this:

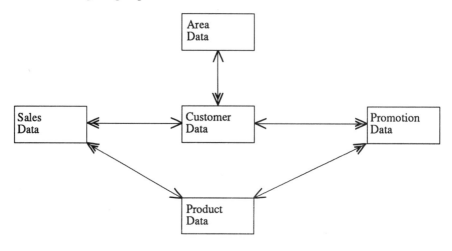

## 4 Analysis

The use of a database, via the medium of direct mail, to support a retail operation, or to complement the activities of a salesman in the field, is a highly targeted form of advertising, based on a knowledge of the *individual* customers that one is trying to reach. Use of a database to select individuals as targets for a direct mail sales offer is, of course, a form of selling. So we have seen examples of the use of database to support two of the classic marketing functions. The third such function is market research, and, to an extent, the wholesale example we discussed above touches on this function too, since this database is being used to analyse customer needs so as to structure an advisory pattern of activity for each salesman. However, a further example of a database being used purely for analysis purposes may help to make the point that in research, as in the other marketing functions, database can play a vital part – whether or not in conjunction with direct mail.

Consider the case of an organization running 300 slimming centres around the country. Some of these establishments are fully residential – but usually short-stay – places, others are simply clubs offering exercise facilities of various sorts, and advice, medical and paramedical for members, all of whom have a common concern – albeit in varying degrees – to lose weight. Members will belong to one only club – clearly close to their home or workplace – but any member may from time to time visit any of the residential establishments, or change the club to which he/she belongs on the occasion of moving house or job.

The clubs offer a variety of regimes of diet and exercise which they try to tailor to the desires, physical condition, and staying power of individual members. The capacity of members to stick with their regimes, once started, is enhanced by group activities, rather after the fashion of Alcoholics Anonymous.

The organization is anxious to monitor the performance of individual clubs, and residential centres, and, indeed the success rate of different regimes. To this end they keep a full computerized record of each member of each club, showing:

Name and address
Club
Date of joining
Weight on joining
Target weight (set by member, with medical agreement)
Date to reach target weight
Prescribed diet
Prescribed exercise
Weekly record of diet
Weekly record of exercise
Weekly weight loss
Medical indications noted
Record of residential visits
Attendance at club
Record from any previous club

This mass of data is analysed regularly in order to see whether there are any significant differences in the success rates achieved by different clubs, and/or by different regimes. (Of course, there are individual factors unknown to the database, such as the extent to which some members cheat and don't tell – but over the large numbers involved this is probably not a statistical problem.)

## 5  Goodwill

Advertising, selling, and market research do not exhaust the list of marketing activities – nor the list of functions in which a marketing database can form a major resource. To quote an example alluded to earlier in this book, a car manufacturer who enables dealers to write regular personalized letters to all the buyers of a particular marque – to advise them of servicing requirements, and other such matters – is not selling, or conducting market research primarily; nor even, except in a secondary sense, advertising. First and foremost, the manufacturer is seeking to cement customer loyalty, to buy goodwill. This is done by indicating that the business knows of this customer as an individual person who bought a car, of a particular model, on a certain date, and who has been running it for just so long since it was last serviced – at which time certain specific items were attended to. It really doesn't much matter whether the dealer's service manager is able to write to Mr Jones in those terms – and to greet him appropriately when he arrives with his vehicle on the appointed day – because the dealer's well-trained memory retains a vivid impression of Mr Jones and his vehicle, down to the last optional extra – or because the manufacturer's computer has regurgitated full details that Monday morning of Jones, Smith, Brown, and Ramsbottom whose cars are all due for servicing that same week. Actually, Mr Jones, who wasn't born yesterday, is perfectly well aware that the latter is the case – but is *still* pleased and comforted by the degree of care and trouble taken to give individual treatment to him, and all the other manufacturer's customers.

# 4 Data Collection

## 1 Sales-Related Data

We looked, in the previous chapter, at some of the problems involved – particularly in a retail environment – in obtaining name and address information from individual customers. For present purposes we will assume that all information arising directly from the database user's dealings with customers – which broadly, if not wholly accurately, we will refer to as sales-related data – is readily available. Nor do we need to become involved in detailed discussion of methods of data capture. But it may be worth saying a few words about some of the consequences of holding sales-related data, which, though they may not be immediately obvious, do require to be recognized and catered for at the start.

**a) Privacy**  Any person or organization that holds, on a computer, personal information about one or more other individuals must, under the terms of the Data Protection Act of 1984, register such related activities with the Data Protection Registrar. For the purposes of the Act, any data that relates to an identifiable individual person is personal data; this means that even a bare list of names and addresses falls within the scope of the Act, when computerized. Registration consists in obtaining a form from the Registrar* and filling it in so as to show the nature of the data held (and/or to be held) and the purposes for which it is, and/or will be, used. To hold personal data on a computer without registering, or to use it in ways that fall outside the terms of registration, is a criminal offence (since 11 May, 1986).

It is therefore to be recommended that the database owner, in registering, specifies not only presently-planned uses of all stored data, but also whatever future uses might reasonably arise. (One

* Mr Eric Howe, Office of the Data Protection Registrar, Springfield House, Water Lane, Wilmslow, Cheshire SK9 5AX.

can of course, amend a registration, or enter a new one, but this minor nuisance can be avoided by some forethought.)

The Data Protection Principles, as enshrined in the Act, are worth quoting, together with the Registrar's own gloss on each. In each case the principle is printed in quotes, with the Registrar's comments below:

"1.  The information to be contained in personal data shall be obtained, and personal data shall be processed, fairly and lawfully."

In considering whether information is obtained fairly, the Registrar will consider whether any person has been deceived or misled as to the purpose for which it is to be held, used, or disclosed.

"2.  Personal data shall be held only for one or more specified and lawful purposes."

Specified purposes are those described on the Register.

"3.  Personal data held for any purpose or purposes shall not be used or disclosed in any manner incompatible with that purpose or those purposes."

Incompatible use or disclosure means otherwise than as described on the Register.

"4.  Personal data held for any purpose or purposes shall be adequate, relevant, and not excessive in relation to that purpose or those purposes."

"5.  Personal data shall be accurate and, where necessary, kept up to date."

"Accurate" means correct and not misleading as to any matter of fact. You may be unable to ensure the accuracy of data received from the Data Subject or a third party. There are provisions in the Act whereby by marking and processing such data appropriately you will not be considered to be in breach of this principle. Such marking or processing will also absolve you from any liability to pay compensation for damage caused by the inaccuracy of the data. Data should be kept up to date except where the purpose for which it is held does not require it to be.

"6.  Personal data held for any purpose or purposes shall not be kept for longer than is necessary for that purpose or those purposes."

"7. An individual shall be entitled:
(a) at reasonable intervals and without undue delay or expense:–
  (i) to be informed by any Data User whether he holds personal data of which that individual is the subject, and
  (ii) to access any such data held by a Data User; and
(b) where appropriate, to have such data corrected or erased."

This principle introduces the right of subject access which is fully described in Section 21 of the Act. "Reasonable intervals" will vary with the nature of the data, the nature and frequency of processing, etc. and is not defined. The Act stipulates that subject access requests shall be met in 40 days after receipt or determination of additional necessary information. The Secretary of State will make an Order fixing the maximum fee which may be charged for subject access, thus ensuring that no "undue expense" is incurred by Data Subjects.

"8. Appropriate security measures shall be taken against unauthorized access to, or alteration, disclosure, or destruction of, personal data, and against accidental loss or destruction of personal data."

In considering whether security measures are appropriate regard should be had to the nature of the personal data and the potential harm which could result from unauthorised access, etc. It will be necessary also to consider the place where data are stored, security measures programmed into the equipment and measures taken for ensuring the reliability of staff having access to the data. This eighth principle applies to Computer Bureaux as well as Data Users.

There are special dispensations for data held for historical and research purposes, where their use is such that it does not cause, or is not likely to cause, damage or distress to any Data Subject. Such data shall not be regarded as unfairly obtained merely because the historical or research purpose was not declared when it was obtained, and it may be kept indefinitely without breaching the sixth principle. Where a breach of any principle comes to the Registrar's attention he may serve a notice requiring you to take steps to comply with the principle or principles in question. Failure to comply with the terms of such a notice will be an offence.

You may feel, as I do, that this is a pretty pointless Act of Parliament, combining the maximum of bureaucratic hair-splitting gobbledeygook, and inconvenience for the trader, with the minimum of intelligible or useful protection for the consumer. Unfortunately this does not make it unique, or even particularly unusual; the Act belongs to a large class of legislation whose object is not so much to achieve anything positive as to remove an irritating and intractable subject from the political agenda. At all events, fourteen years after the setting up of the first (Younger) committee on the subject, the Act has reached the statute book, and must be heeded. Copies of the Act may be acquired from HM Stationery Office. However, a mere reading of the Act, necessary as that is, will raise more questions than it answers; a great deal will depend upon how the Act is interpreted – in the first instance by the Registrar's office, and subsequently by the Courts. The Registrar has issued sundry pamphlets of explanation and elaboration; these can be obtained from his office. The Advertising Association has also published (with the approval of the Registrar) in March 1987 a Code of Practice "Covering the Use of Personal Data for Advertising and Direct Marketing Purposes". Copies may be obtained (and should be by all readers of this book) from the Association, price £1.50.

The general expectation of those who have studied the Act, and discussed its implications with the Registrar, originally was that the Act was not likely to interfere substantially with normal accepted practice within the direct marketing industry *provided that* the purposes for which personal data is used were fully covered by the terms of registration. However, anyone collecting personal data which he or she intends (or might in future wish) to disclose to a third party – e.g. in a list rental, or list swop arrangement – does need to consider the implications of the first principle with particular care, and should give close attention to the AA's code of practice on this subject. During the second half of 1988 the Registrar's office began to concern itself more closely with the concept of "fair" collection and use of data within the first principle. At the time of writing a prolonged debate is in progress between the industry (represented by the Data Protection Committee of the Advertising Association) and the Registrar on this subject, and it would appear that in the outcome more stringent duties are likely to be laid on data users than the AA's Code of Practice currently enjoins. The Registrar's interpretation of the Act is that personal data should only be used by a data user with the "informed consent" of the data subject, and that this means full disclosure of the uses to which data will, or may, be put, at the time of collection. The implications of such an interpretation for the wide variety of different methods of data collection are the subject of current discussions. The Registrar's view of the matter is contained in the now notorious Guideline 19 issued by his office; since this document is impossible of literal implementation, it does appear probable that it will be modified, or further "interpreted" at some time in the near future. Meanwhile, the AA's Data Protection Committee can advise on the best means for an individual to protect his position in his own particular circumstances. A fairly typical example of the sort of foolish confusion that arises when the law attempts to intervene in matters which are no part of its proper concern.

**b) Duplication**   Most organizations that collect individual customer information are obliged to identify customers by reference simply to name and address. Banks, insurance companies, and a few others, are fortunate in being able, most of the time, to rely on account numbers, policy numbers, and so on: others lack this advantage. Names and addresses are notoriously hard to handle, being liable to numerous human errors in transcription, and – in the case of addresses at least – often not written the same way twice running. As a consequence, a single customer is liable to have his or her name and address recorded twice, thrice, or four times, with variations, on a single database. Where the database is being used to generate communications, such an occurrence on any large scale is a disaster, resulting in wasted costs, and customer irritation – as well as destroying just that sense of individual attention which the mailer wishes to engender. And even where the purpose of the database is primarily statistical, wholly misleading results may follow.

All of this makes duplication a major headache. A strategy for dealing with it has to be decided on right at the start of data collection, if the ensuing problems are to be kept within bounds. The problem is basically this: when the database receives notice that a sale has been made to Mrs X living at such and such an address, how does the computer decide whether this is the first record of Mrs X, or whether the database already holds a record for her?

A whole variety of logical systems (going under the horrible generic title of merge-purge systems) exist for examining names and addresses in order to determine whether they belong to the same person or not, and these logical systems are incorporated in computer programmes. These can then be used either by a service bureau, which will take 1, 2, 3,...n files of names and addresses and match them together, eliminating duplicates both within and between files, or by a database user, to determine in relation to each incoming name and address in turn whether or not it is already present on the database. All of these systems are to a greater or lesser extent imperfect: there is, after all, no logical method available for determining whether:

J.A.C. Smith
12 Laburnum Grove
Newbury
Berks.

is or is not the same person as:

Arthur Smith
Dunrovin
Laburnum Grove
Newbury
Berks.

unless access can be had to further extraneous information. (And this is only one of an immense range of potential ambiguities.) So that all systems that rely on the content of names and addresses alone must end by "taking a view" – just as a clerk would in a similar situation, with the major difference being that a clerk's "view" will tend to differ from one occasion to the next, whereas a computer will at least be consistent – and this "view" will in some circumstances result in two separate customers being treated as one, and in others will create two separate records for the same person.

The safest system for the avoidance of duplication lies in the use of postcodes. A single postcode embraces, on average, 15 households, so that the appearance in an address of a correct postcode already gives a high degree of discrimination. But how to be sure that the postcode *is* correct – bearing in mind that customers misquote them, and staff mistranscribe them? Well, again there are computer bureaux that undertake to postcode files of names and addresses by reference to the Postal Address File (PAF) created, and maintained, by the Post Office. And the same rules used by the bureau for this purpose can be incorporated in database maintenance programmes by any database user to deal with single name and address transactions.

Postcoding has a number of advantages:

i) It makes deduplication of addresses (names are another matter) simple: every valid address in the country is represented once and only once on the PAF; if an address can be found on the PAF, it will always give rise to the same postcode; if an address cannot be found on the PAF the implication must normally be that the address given is incorrect.

ii) Within limits, addresses can be corrected by reference to the PAF: missing towns or counties, and sometimes districts, can be added and a wide range of mis-spellings corrected. Some of these corrections will improve the deliverability, or speed of delivery, of the mail; all of them will help improve the general presentation and image of the mailing piece.

iii) Addresses that cannot be found on the PAF, and cannot be corrected, will be output for clerical scrutiny – preventing incorrect, and perhaps undeliverable, items from reaching and corrupting the database.

iv) Under the Post Office's new bulk mailing system, Mailsort, postal rebate or discount will only be available to mailers who achieve a high level of postcoding on their outgoing mail. (See further in Chapter 5, Section 4 below.)

v) As we shall see in the next section, the postcode is the key to externally available demographic data about addresses throughout the country, which may be of marketing value.

The postcode, then, narrows an address down to approximately 15 households. Adding to that postcode a house number will define the household virtually uniquely.* A database that uses the postcode as its prime household identifier, that allows no un-postcoded records on the database, and that checks all incoming addresses, already postcoded or not, against the PAF, will ensure that no duplicate, and no incorrect, addresses can appear on the database, ever. (As always, there have to be exceptions. It is by no means unknown for new housing estates, or individual houses, to be occupied before postcodes are assigned, and certainly before the new postcodes have been added to the PAF. Clearly some allowance must be made for

---

*Theoretically ambiguities are still possible – but in a trivial number of cases, e.g. where a postcode covers a part of two streets so that 1 High Street and 1 Church Street could share the same postcode. This happens in one or two areas where postcoding was erroneously handled at the outset.

such circumstances, short of refusing to recognize the existence of the households concerned.)

The database user must still decide what he wants to do about duplication of surnames. Are Mr and Mrs Smith, living at the same address, to be treated as one person (i.e. to be allotted one only record on file) or as two? What about A.C. Smith and J.A. Smith? Or indeed, is the system to allow two different surnames to exist at the same address? In fact, is the basic record in the database a person or a household (i.e.for practical purposes a postal delivery point)? And if a household, can it, like a real household, contain multiple persons? And if so, what are the limitations?

The answers to these questions will vary with the nature of the business that the database exists to serve. The point of posing them here is simply to indicate that there is a good deal of planning regarding the basic structure of the information one wishes to hold, that needs to precede the collection of database information. Many of the problems of database structure are technical problems, which we will not attempt to deal with in this book. But the questions arising from problems of duplication, and how to overcome them, are fundamental to the marketing objectives of the database user: they are a good deal too important to be left to the "experts".

c) **Expansion**  Data, like the universe itself, is in a state of continual expansion – and at a very similar speed, as it sometimes seems. The problems that arise from this are not primarily problems of storing data, since the storage capacity of computers has at least kept pace in recent years with the growth in data to be stored. Nor is there a problem in accessing individual pieces of stored data: today's computer systems are well-adapted to this purpose. Rather the problem occurs when very large, and continually increasing volumes of data require to be sequentially accessed – for example for analysis purposes. Even with the processing speeds achieved by today's equipment, the amount of work required, and the time taken by it can, with an expanding database, quickly overwhelm the computer.

The consequence of this is that, in any given marketing application, there is likely to be a need first to settle for recording something less than the total available information, and second to accept that stored data, after some lapse of time, can be deleted, or subsumed into a summary. Let us consider an example of each process.

A company is selling a range of units for fitted bedrooms, kitchens, bathrooms. It has in its range 150 different units. Units are available in (on average) 4 different sets of dimensions, 8 different finishes, and 10 different styles. Now, what is to be the basic product building block under which we record marketing data? If we record full data about each sale, we have potentially 48,000 product variants. Moreover, a given style lasts on average for two years, and is then replaced – giving an additional 24,000 items a year. Does the marketing department truly require to record and analyse each individual sale according to one of 48,000 current variants, plus a growing number of past ones? Or can we settle for coding our products, so far as the marketing database is concerned, by unit and style only, giving a mere 1,500 possibilities, and an extra 750 a year?

Indeed, do we need to keep past sales records, at this level of detail, indefinitely? Could we not, once a given style goes out of use, simply summarize the sales data pertaining to it under the 150 basic units – which are fewer in number and subject to much less frequent change?

Clearly the answers to questions of this kind will vary with each individual case. The important point is that this question must be asked early on, before data collection starts: what are the basic building blocks of data that will be used in our database structure? Are they:

the household?
the individual person within the household?
the basic product?
the individual product variant?
the region, or branch?
the individual salesman, or assistant, in a region/branch?

To get answers that will stand the test of time demands the utmost co-operation, understanding and mutual respect between those – the marketing staff – for whose use the database is being built, and the construction team of systems people. It is because these qualities of understanding and respect are so frequently, and sadly lacking, and because, consequently, serious co-operation is often not forthcoming, that so many database enterprises turn out to be either substantial disasters, or much harder work and much greater generators of frustration in their later stages than they need be if properly planned at the beginning. We will revert to this theme at a later stage in this book.

## 2   Demographic Data

Ideally, the marketing person who has absorbed the admonition, Know Your Customer, wants as much information as is available about past customers and about future prospects, as individuals. We have already seen the need to preserve the data available within the company on sales and promotions; we will see in the next section what additional individual data can be obtained, and how. But here we will first consider the acquisition and use of statistical data, relating not to individuals but to groups.

During the last ten years a number of companies have started to offer demographic data, and/or demographic services, which are alleged to be capable of improving the targeting, and hence the cost-effectiveness, of a very wide variety of marketing efforts. If these companies are to be believed, the intelligent use of demographics can guide a user in choosing the optimum site for a new store, in deciding what products to stock in a given area, in maximizing response to a promotion, whether in the press or by mail, in planning distribution systems or allocating sales territories. Our purpose here is to examine the origins, development, and present status of demographic systems; to indicate what types of system are on offer; to discuss the similarities and differences of competing systems, and to give some evaluation of the claims made for demographics as a marketing tool.

Demographic data is, simply, statistical information about population groups. It is extremely important to bear this in mind: although some of the systems we shall examine do use some information about individual persons or households, the basis of them all is the group. Information about the group can be ascribed to individuals in it only on the basis of probability. Thus, if we know that 35% of the people in a given group are retired, we also know that the chance of any one individual in that group being retired is slightly better than 1 in 3. And we know that a promotion directed to retired persons will be 250% more effective in reaching its target if addressed to this group rather than to a similar sized group of which only 10% are retired. What we must *not* do is to think of the first group as though it consisted solely, or even mainly, of retired persons, since 65% of it does not.

Of course, in an ideal marketing world, we would have a wealth of available information about individuals. In the real world, collection of such information across a population of 43 million adults (or 20 million households) is inordinately expensive. What we do have, readily, cheaply, and plentifully, is information about groups. The most plentiful source of such information in the UK is the decennial census.

**a) The census**   The last UK census was taken in 1981. Every householder is obliged by law to complete a census form; the data from these forms is collated by the Office of Population Censuses and

Surveys (OPCS). Clearly no data for individual households is available from OPCS. However, responsibility for collecting census forms lies with an army of enumerators, each of whom deals with a small geographic area containing an average of 150 households and known as an enumeration district (ED). The ED is the smallest available building block of census data: anyone can buy from OPCS a library of magnetic tapes containing full census data about the 130,000 EDs in England, Scotland, and Wales. (Northern Ireland is excluded from consideration here: its data at the 1981 census was very imperfectly collected; this, added to differences in presentation, make it extremely difficult to interpret. The systems considered here do not deal with it, unless on a one-off basis for a particular client.)

This data is broadly of three kinds. It describes:
  i) the people who live in the ED: total numbers, numbers by age band and by marital status, for example;
  ii) socio-economic conditions, such as numbers in certain types of occupation; levels of car ownership, etc.;
  iii) types of housing.

The amount of data available is very large indeed: for each of the 130,000 EDs there are some 4,000 variables, or pieces of data, plus a further 1,500 that apply only to parts of the country (e.g. Scotland, Wales). Before we discuss how this mass of information can be reduced to manageable proportions, it may be sensible to pause and consider in what basic ways this type of data about groups of households can be used in a marketing context.

The root problem of all marketing effort is the problem of targeting: whom are we trying to reach? This problem underlies the siting of a new shop, the stocking of a range of products, the placing of a newspaper or TV advertisement, the sending of a direct mail promotion. Targeting means ensuring that our message reaches as many as possible of the people we are interested in, while wasting the least possible effort in reaching people we are not interested in. So the object of looking at information that describes groups of people is to be able to differentiate one group from another: what we hope is that differences in the demographic make-up of groups will be reflected in differences in all types of purchasing behaviour. We must begin, then, by establishing population groups that are demographically different; we can then consider how to test any marketing hypotheses about those groups.

On the other hand, our chosen population groups, whatever their demographic differences, must not be so small that observed behavioural differences between them have no statistical significance.

An example may help. Suppose we were to use 130,000 EDs as our population groups, and were then to apply to those groups data from a random national survey of 30,000 consumers showing what brand of toilet soap they habitually bought. The majority of EDs would not contain any person from our survey; those that did would have one or two persons. It would therefore be impossible, from this survey data, to use the demographic differences between EDs as a way of differentiating peoples' purchasing behaviour regarding toilet soap. If, however, we had only 30 population groups instead of 130,000, then each group would contain on average 1,000 persons from our survey, and this should be enough to observe differences in brand preferences between groups with different demographic characteristics.

The first problem, then, is to band together EDs with similar demographic profiles so as to form groups whose demography is significantly different each from the other, and whose populations are sufficiently large that even quite modest research samples will show up at significant levels within each of them.

But before we can do this there is another problem: 4,000 variables is far too large a mass of data to handle for each ED – the more so when we recognize that much of the data is either of no interest for marketing purposes, or repetitive. All demographic systems therefore begin by reducing this number to a more manageable total of significant items. These pieces of data are then expressed proportionally – e.g.:

Proportion of ED residents aged 15-24
Proportion of permanent dwellings rented unfurnished

The systems we shall be looking at use variously 41, 104, 38, and 65 principal items of data from among the 4,000 census variables.

Having determined which census variables to use, the demographic system will then examine how best, by reference to these variables, the 130,000 EDs can be banded together in groups whose members have broadly similar characteristics. The four systems we will be looking at derive (by a computerized statistical process known as cluster analysis) 38, 60, 58, or 150 groups respectively of EDs. In all four cases these groups can be further aggregated into smaller numbers of super-groups.

So we now have a limited number of groups of EDs, where each group has a substantial population, and all the EDs in each group have broadly similar demographic profiles as determined by the most significant of the census variables. So far, so good.

**b) Enumeration districts and postcodes**   One serious theoretical problem remains. Let us suppose that a marketing manager possesses data – from market research sources or whatever – about the behaviour of a number of people. He wishes to relate this behaviour to the known demographic characteristics of the areas in which these people live, in order to see whether demography is a significant predictor of this particular behaviour. How does he discover in which ED each person in his survey lies?

The key to this whole process is the postcode: if we know an individual's postcode (for which we have a map reference) then we can "allocate" him or her to an ED (for which we also have a map reference). However, the migration from postcode to ED is not easy. The average postcode comprises 15 households – i.e. there are 10 average postcodes to the average ED. But the boundaries of each have been allocated independently; consequently a postcode area may well lie in more than one ED.* As we shall see, different systems use different methods to relate the two entities; there is as yet no perfect answer. All systems end up by allocating each and every postcode to an ED, and hence to a group of EDs with a common demographic profile. By this means a demographic profile can be assigned to any individual household in the country. It does need to be stressed again that there is no guarantee that that profile will be in any way accurate for that household: if we say that a given address falls in a neighbourhood of "Private Houses, Well-Off Elderly" it may still be the case that every member of that household belongs to the 40% of people in that neighbourhood who are under 45: the neighbourhood description deals only in relativities, and indicates merely that well-off elderly people living in private houses are characteristic of this neighbourhood.

**c) Additional data**   All four systems considered here use, sometimes in different ways, further data. Some of this data, unlike the census statistics, is about individual persons; it is broadly of two types:

i)   *Sample data*   There is a wide range of market research data available, from such sources as the Target Group Index (TGI) or the Financial Research Survey (FRS). This indicates the relationship of a sample of individuals to one or more items in which the survey is interested. Thus, FRS will tell us who, and what proportion, of a national sample are shareholders;

---

* Except in Scotland, where things are organized, as ever, more logically. Possibly at the 1991 census a touch of logic will arrive south of the border.

by allocating these individuals to their appropriate ED groups, based on their postcodes, we can determine whether one ED group holds significantly more shareholders than another.

ii) *Universal data*   Above all the electoral register, which tells us the names of the individuals who live in each ED (via their postcodes). The next most frequently-encountered example is the Lord Chancellor's list – of County Court judgements, satisfactions, Bills of Sale, and bankruptcies. Since all of these phenomena are recorded on the list, it is possible to know the total number occurring in each ED, or group of EDs.

Finally, it is possible to obtain information about road networks and journey times which can be related to the areas in which people live. This can be used to indicate how many people, in what groups of EDs, live within a given area, or within a given journey time of a particular spot. A major value in linking demographics to postal geography consists in the ability to take virtually any data that can be mapped and to express it in a way that relates to population – and to population groups differentiated by demographic characteristics. What we must now consider, first as a general principle, and then separately for each of the methodologies in use, is whether the differentiation given by clustering enumeration districts on the basis of census variables can in fact produce usefully differentiated markets for products and services.

**d) Overview of theory**   There are a number of reasons for being sceptical about the concept of using demographics in this way:

i) Most obvious of these is the fact that a census happens only once every ten years. At the time of writing the 1981 census data is already seven years old; the 1991 data will not be available in these systems till late 1993, by which time the 1981 data will be twelve years old; since it is generally reckoned that some 12% of the population moves house every year, it is clear that after 12 years we are not looking at anything like the same population in the same place as represented by the census. How much this matters will vary from one application to another. Clearly EDs in which significant numbers of new houses (and even 15 houses constitutes 10% of the average ED) have been built since 1981, will be incorrectly described by census data. The sale of council houses, which only started in the 1980s, has substantially swollen the ranks of owner-occupiers. City centre EDs can change their demography radically in a few years – through slum clearance, or by gentrification. Areas which had, in 1981, a high proportion of children aged 0-4 (e.g. new housing estates, or new towns) are likely to show different characteristics five and more years later. And so on.

ii) As noted already, there is a theoretical problem with the central function of relating postcodes to EDs, caused by the non-coincidence of their boundaries. The real problem is worse: the whole process of matching depends upon using the Central Postcode Directory (CPD), which gives a grid reference for every postcode, in conjunction with grid references for EDs. Difficulties arise in three ways:

First: The CPD map references are imprecise: they define only a square on the ground of 100 x 100 metres. In the case where one or more ED boundaries run through this square, a postcode can be allocated to an ED in which no part of it actually falls. This can be shown to affect up to 50% of the postcodes in city centres. (The effect is less where EDs are geographically larger.)

Second: A substantial number of CPD map references are actually wrong, due to mistranscription of data and careless or non-existent verification. This can result in postcodes being allocated to EDs not just yards, but many miles, astray.

Third: While the GLC, before its demise, had produced digitized grid references for the boundaries of all its EDs, no such information exists outside London. Although ED maps exist, the only digital reference for EDs is a grid reference for the centroid of each. This means that the computer system, when allocating a non-London postcode to "its" ED, must choose the ED with the nearest centroid to the (imprecise) grid reference of the postcode. Since EDs do not have regular shapes, this causes more errors.

It is extremely hard to assess how much difference these problems make in practice. Where a postcode, for instance, is allocated to the ED next door to its "true" ED (certainly much the most common error) the probability is that the two EDs are sufficiently similar to end up in the same cluster anyway – in which case no harm is done. For the future, work is in hand to enhance and correct the CPD – which will benefit all systems discussed here – and since ED boundaries will have to be

re-drawn for 1991, it may be possible to make them co-termin-
ous with postcodes throughout the UK. However, the vast job
of digitizing ED boundaries will still have to be done if perfect
matching is to be achieved.

These are serious theoretical problems, but, in the last analysis
marketing is a pragmatic art rather than a theoretical science: the
real test of this methodology is how well it works in practice.
Beyond doubt it has worked well for some users; it is also capable
of very considerable improvement; ultimately however it is liable
to be limited by the ageing of its base data.

**e) Overview of practice**  There are a number of different kinds of
marketing purpose for which demographic systems can be used.

i) Owners of a list of names and addresses can have the codes
for demographic clusters (as determined by one system or
another – or even more than one) added to each record on
their files, and can use these codes as a discriminating factor
(on their own or in conjunction with other data) to determine
whether or not to mail individuals with a particular offer. It is
in practice unlikely that the very generalized and imprecise
data underlying these codes will make more than a marginal
difference to the particular and precise information that list
owners should have about their own customers. But circumstances can alter cases. There can be no harm, and only
small cost, in mounting a test to discover whether the extra
discrimination offered by one of these systems results in extra
response.

ii) Users of an outside list on which there is little discriminatory
information except codes for demographic clusters, may use
this data to choose groups of people to mail. They may determine which clusters to use by one of a variety of methods:
Either: Subjectively, by looking at the demographic profile of
each cluster and comparing it with their knowledge of
their own product.
Or: By taking a profile of their own customers, to see which
clusters they preponderately fall into, and choosing from
those. (There is danger of a circularity in this method. If,
for example, it is found that a user's customers come
dominantly from "affluent suburban housing" this may
mean merely that he or she has been advertising exclusively in media confined to such households. This own-list-
profile method will work properly only if the source from

which that list was recruited is compatible with the list being researched.)

Or: By running a test to a sample of the proposed list, and seeing whether response is conditioned by the clusters in which promotees live.

This is one of the most frequent uses of demographics to date, so let us pause and consider it. There is no question but that all four systems surveyed do succeed in creating population clusters with widely differing demographic profiles. There is also ample evidence that a wide range of purchasing behaviour is significantly different from one cluster to another. What these statistically significant differences amount to in terms of profit and loss is another matter. Let us try a hypothetical example.*

There were, in 1982, 1,524,000 readers of *The Guardian*. Allocating a representative sample of these readers to the ED clusters produced by one particular demographic system indicated that the cluster categorized as "High status non-family areas" scored 271 for *Guardian* readers, against a national average of 100, or a penetration of 9% against 3.5%. Suppose that we have a product known to be attractive to *Guardian* readers; we mail the 1,874,000 households known to be in this cluster, knowing we will reach 169,000 *Guardian* readers. Let us further suppose that the response pattern is:

| | | | |
|---|---|---|---|
| *Guardian* readers | :5% | = | 8,450 |
| Others | :1% | = | 17,050 |
| | | | 25,500 = 1.36% |

If we had mailed a similar number of households from random EDs containing an average number of *Guardian* readers (i.e. 65,590) we would have achieved:

| | | | |
|---|---|---|---|
| *Guardian* readers | :5% | = | 3,280 |
| Others | :1% | = | 18,084 |
| | | | 21,364 = 1.14% |

Now, the difference between 1.14 and 1.36 could represent a lot of money, or even the difference between profit and loss

---

* Data used in this example is derived from application of a 1982 NRS survey to Acorn Groups.

– it is, after all, a 19% difference. The improvement may, or may not, be sufficient to pay for the costs incurred. But it isn't anything like as large as the difference between 271 and 100, or between 9% and 3.5%. The reason for this, of course, is that the phenomenon at which we are looking is only a fairly small part of the whole. If we had an ED cluster in which *Guardian* readers had a 90% penetration, against a national average of 35%, then, on the same assumptions, the difference in response would be 4.5% versus 2.3% – an improvement this time of 96%.

Each potential user of a demographic system will have to do his own sums, and to look not merely at the relative discriminatory power of this or that system, but at the absolute number of real prospects it will deliver, and at the cost of reaching them.

Finally, it would appear that demographic systems are rather better at distinguishing bad marketing prospects than good ones. To return to the 1982 National Readership Survey, households of Social Grade A have, unsurprisingly, a score of 1 in "Poorest Council Estates" compared to a norm of 100. Yet the highest ED cluster achieved a score in this context of only 253. One of the highest scores in the whole survey was 367, for households with oil-fired central heating in "Agricultural Areas"; yet another cluster had a low score of 17 – one-sixth of the norm. This is probably just a way of stating the fairly obvious – that poor areas are more homogeneous than affluent areas – but it has implications for demographic marketing which are worth thinking about.

iii) Demographic systems were first developed in this country for direct mail use. But in recent years other uses – for some of which they may be far more valuable than for direct mail – have been developed. Some of these uses – such as optimal siting of a new store – are highly specific; others are about offering a deeper insight into the nature and composition of one's market – a benefit that may be hard to quantify, but that no marketing person would turn down out of hand.

The general principle is that one can define a geographic area in a number of different ways – as a collection of postcodes, or postcode sectors, or enumeration districts; as everything within a certain radius of a given point, or anywhere within a certain journey time of such a point; by county, or local authority, or constituency, or ward, or TV region – and any or all of these can be related via grid references and postcodes to the people who live in these geographic expressions. Through market research surveys, existing or specially commissioned, one can characterize the buying habits of people in these areas against the national norm and subdivide by demographic clusters if required. One can map the propensity of people in urban or rural areas to travel for their shopping: the more expensive the product, the farther people travel for it; wealthier people travel longer distances for more things than poorer people. None of this is surprising, but being able to express it in precise numerical terms, and to plot its incidence on a map, is new.

From this welter of data one can draw all manner of inferences about shopping patterns; these may help determine policy on the siting of a store, or become ammunition in discussing rental levels. They are certainly a basis for a scientific approach to optimizing stock-holdings of different lines.

In sum then, I am not an enthusiast for including demographic data, or codes, on advertisers' own customer files – certainly not without testing their value first. For lists devoid of other discriminants, demographic clusters are an advance on nothing: whether the advance is great enough to recoup the cost is an open question, whose answer will vary from case to case: again it can be tested. In non-direct mail situations, as an aid to defining market areas or giving an insight into market characteristics, I believe demographics have a great deal to offer.

That, however, is a generalized picture: when we turn to specific systems we will see that one practitioner or another has taken this or that approach in an attempt to eradicate, or lessen, some of the problems alluded to above. I am not sure that matters will change greatly between now and 1993; I am confident there will be considerable advances in the mid-1990s, and that those who have gained experience in the meantime will be the first to benefit.

**f) Acorn** (an acronym for A Classification Of Residential Neighbourhoods) is a demographic system offered by CACI – an international consultancy founded in the USA in 1962. CACI was not, as its literature claims, "the first to obtain (census statistics) from the census office" which they did in 1977 some years after Reader's Digest had taken this route. They were however the first company to use these statistics to build a generalized system that could provide a national demographic profile. The other systems discussed below have all built on CACI's experience – although each has added something of its own.

The current Acorn system dates from 1983, and uses the 1981 census statistics. From among the 4,000 census variables, Acorn uses 40 in order to group the 130,000 EDs, by a process of cluster analysis, into 38 "neighbourhood types", which further coalesce into 11 "groups". CACI offers the following range of services, connected more or less closely with Acorn:

i) *Acorn profiling* CACI will take a random sample of a client's own postcoded list of customers (minimum sample size 5,000), apply Acorn codes to each record, and provide a profile of that sample indicating what proportion of its total falls within each Acorn type, compared with the generality of the population. This exercise can give a valuable insight into the make-up of one's customer list. It *may* also help in deciding how to structure future marketing campaigns (but see the comments in e.ii above).

Sub-profiles of groups of separately-identified names within the total sample can also be provided at the same time (minimum no. 2,000). Cost of such an exercise would be not less than £1,000 (1987 prices) for 5,000 names, plus 20% per sub-analysis.

ii) *Acorn test mailing* CACI will take a list of postcoded addresses and separate them according to Acorn codes which the client has selected for mailing and those that have not been selected. Codes will be added to the selected records on this file, which is returned to the client, only for the purpose of analysing the response. Cost will be £2.50 per 1,000 records input, plus £10 per thousand records mailed (minimum £500).

iii) *Acorn coding* CACI will lease to a client the Acorn directory, so that permanent Acorn codes can be added to the client's own postcoded file. The client can then analyse, by Acorn type, any customer behaviour recorded on the file. Minimum lease term is three years; there is a fixed annual charge plus a price per 1,000 records on the client's file. Automatic annual directory updates are supplied (e.g where the Post Office changes postcodes).

iv) *The Acorn list* CACI offer selections from the 43 million electoral register, as computerized and postcoded by UAPT-Infolink – a leading credit reference agency. This list is Acorn coded, therefore Acorn-based selections are possible. Cost of renting this list for one-time use is £60 per thousand names (minimum order 10,000) with reducing rates for increasing volumes.

Possession of this list also enables CACI to select "neighbours" of a client's existing customers – those who live in adjacent houses, or the same street. Cost as above, plus a fee per thousand client records for whom neighbours are supplied.

v) *Spectra* This is a relatively new service offered by CACI, and described as a direct mail response improvement system. The initial part of the process is not very different from the Acorn profiling described above: simply it uses more data, of a kind chosen to meet the specific needs of each client, in order to provide an individual model of a market, instead of using merely the generalized Acorn segmentation.

Spectra starts with a postcoded sample of client addresses about each of which we have either a yes/no variable (they have/have not responded to a given offer) or a continuous variable (they have spent x pounds in the last year). Any further available client data will be added to this file – purchase data, accounting data, etc. Also added will be CACI data – Acorn codes, individual census variables, travel data, retail data. From this mixture of data Spectra will produce a profile showing what factors affect response, and will then calculate a "score" for each record on the client's file: the higher the score the greater the propensity to respond. The culmination of this process is a "gains chart" which shows how the "best" 10%, next best 10% etc of the file will respond.

vi) *Site* This system enables a CACI client to define one or more geographic areas; Site will then produce for each area population statistics broken down by Acorn type, details of local workforce, unemployment statistics, and a profile of households derived from the census data. This system can also produce a quantification of the local market for goods or services across 15 standard retail fields.

vii) *Local expenditure zones* CACI has divided the UK into 1,100 LEZs each with a shopping centre and crown post office. For any LEZ CACI can provide reports as for Site (see above) together with an analysis of sales potential for any product, an estimate of total market size, and details of retail competition.

viii) *Drive time zones* CACI has modelled the main road network so as to facilitate calculation of journey times,and esti-
mation of numbers of persons (categorized by Acorn) within
x minutes of a given point.

ix) *Door-to-door* CACI will define postal sectors that best meet
a client's definition of Acorn types to be targeted. This definition can then be used by a door-to-door distributor – an
improvement on blanket coverage.

x) *Monica* CACI has pioneered a system for estimating the
likely age group of an individual from his/her first name.
This system is claimed to give a good age indication for 75%
of UK adults, and to add therefore to discriminatory potential
on the electoral register.

**g) Pinpoint** Pinpoint Analysis Ltd. is a small independent company
which was the first to challenge (in 1983) the early monopoly in
demographic systems held by CACI. Its primary product is PIN
(Pinpoint Identification of Neighbourhoods) which attempts, like
Acorn, to group enumeration districts with like census characteristics
in clusters, and to assign to them postcode areas, using the Central
Postcode Directory (CPD) as a link.

Pinpoint was the first to point to the extent of error arising from
the use of the CPD. (See para d.ii above for details.) Pinpoint is
now playing the leading role in correcting the CPD (where this is
feasible) and hopes to go further by producing an accurate grid
reference for every household in the country (Pinpoint Address
Code, or PAC). This, if done as promised, will effectively by-pass
the CPD, and possibly the whole postcode system (although the
problem of precise definition of ED boundaries will still exist).
Correction of the CPD benefits all current systems equally; grid-
referencing houses will be a further significant enhancement.

Pinpoint in its early days made a lot of noise about the inaccuracies
of earlier ED/postcode linkages. It is probable that they ascribed
too great an importance to these inaccuracies, and that their claim
to have a system that, by correcting (some of) these inaccuracies
was greatly superior to Acorn was too sweeping. Moreover, it is
doubtful if any system's methodology in this linking area is *now*
inferior to any other's. However the dismissive attitudes struck by
Pinpoint's competitors are too reminiscent of the treatment of the
little boy who insisted on remarking that the emperor was insuffi-
ciently clad. Pinpoint does have an obsession with precise accuracy
of data, and although that may be costly for them, it can't be bad

for their clients. And it is this drive for precision that is behind PAC, which could be a real benefit to demographic users.

The standard PIN classification began with 104 census variables, selected judgementally from the 4,000 total. These were subjected to a principal components analysis, and the first ten principal components were selected. These in turn were used in a cluster analysis against all 130,000 EDs to produce 60 ED clusters, which in turn reduce to 25, or twelve, super-clusters.

The basic services offered by Pinpoint are:

i) *Postcoding* Pinpoint is one of the Post Office approved suppliers of computerized postcoding services; as such it is able to postcode client files and to obtain for clients financial assistance from the Post Office.

ii) *Profiling* Pinpoint will profile a sample of a client's file against the standard PIN codes. The process is analogous to Acorn profiling (f.ii above). Cost of profiling 10,000 names would vary from £800-£2,000 depending on precise requirements.

iii) *Test mailings and prospect scoring* Again as with Acorn, Pinpoint can code a list of names for a test mailing, and can analyse the results of the test to "score" the master list from which the test names were taken.

iv) *PIN directory* Alternatively, PIN codes can be added to all records on a client file, either through Pinpoint itself, on a once-for-all basis, or through the lease of the PIN directory for use on the client's own main frame. (Cost, £25,000 for a lease to expire in 1993.)

v) *Electoral register* Pinpoint does not itself own a computerized electoral register, but has an exclusive arrangement with Grattans, who do. Names can be supplied from PIN-selected areas.

vi) *Finpin* This is the first of what is planned as a series of specialized systems for specific market sectors – in this case the financial sector. Finpin starts with market research data from 65,000 interviews conducted by Financial Research Services (FRS – an NOP subsidiary). This data is applied to the census information to identify 58 significant census variables; these are subjected to a principal components analysis which produces 20 principal components; these are used in a cluster analysis to provide 40 ED clusters, which in turn coalesce into 10 or 4 super-clusters. Pinpoint claim that, while PIN is a powerful general-purpose discriminator, Finpin is very much more powerful in relation to financial products; there is certainly evidence of this in particular cases. Finpin can be used in all the same ways as PIN itself; its directory costs £30,000 to lease.

vii) *Individual analyses*   The trend of Pinpoint's development has been towards the provision of individually specific analyses for individual clients – with sector-specific analyses like Finpin being a sort of half-way house. Pinpoint claims to be unique in holding all 5,500 census variables on-line for all of the 130,000 EDs to which each applies; the company can thus build a new cluster system to conform to the needs of a particular client, using any collection of variables considered relevant; it can rank EDs on the basis of any one of the 10 principal components derived by PIN (e.g. the Wealth component – a combination of census variables tending to indicate wealth) or the 20 derived by Finpin, or on the basis of a single census variable (e.g. percentage of children 0-15).

viii) *CENTRY*   This is a general purpose piece of software designed to ease the production of some of these individual analyses. It is in fact an area profiling system: it allows the user to define his own area, of any size or shape, and to obtain a report showing the occurrence of any combination of census variables – with comparisons either against the UK, or another defined area. Centry allows the user to work from a terminal in his/her office on-line to the Pinpoint hardware.

ix)   *Retail potential reports*   Pinpoint uses Family Expenditure Survey (FES) data from the Department of Employment to estimate consumer spending by type of shop and type of goods/services. This estimate can be made for any defined area; the cost of each report is £95, or £150 if a Centry demographic report is taken at the same time.

x)   *Lupin*   This is a database consisting of the results of 60,000 telephone interviews to establish consumer shopping patterns. The survey covers 60% of the country, taking 1 in 200 telephone subscribers in each area covered. Using this data, plus information about store locations and sizes, a variety of models can be built to illustrate shopping patterns and to predict the effects of openings/closures.

xi) *Mapping*  Pinpoint's greatest area of specialization is in mapping; while all four systems have mapping capability, Pinpoint believes deeply in the virtues of expressing all manner of data on physical maps; it can produce these in the form of translucent overlays.

**h) Mosaic**  This system is an offering of CCN Systems Ltd., a subsidiary of Great Universal Stores (GUS). In origin CCN was a credit reference bureau for GUS, and this still underlies much of what they offer. Today, however, the company is a large supplier of services, particularly computer-based services, in direct marketing.

Mosaic has two fundamental differences from the other three systems considered in this paper. First, it is not based on enumeration districts, but on postcodes; instead of allocating postcodes to EDs and then clustering EDs with like characteristics, Mosaic ascribes ED census data to the postcodes that are held to lie in each ED, and then clusters the postcodes that have like characteristics. So far this sounds like a distinction without a difference – and so it would be but for the second factor: Mosaic incorporates into its clustering system information from non-census sources that is available at postcode, or at household (aggregated to postcode) level.

Thus, other systems have available judgement summons information; they can use this, for example, to screen out from a mailing list pre-selected by demographics, individuals with judgements against them. Mosaic, however, is unique in incorporating area data about judgement summonses into the classification system itself. This raises legal and ethical issues (on which CCN have wisely sought OFT advice). To screen out an individual person against whom a judgement has been entered, is unexceptionable. To choose not to send a mailing to an area in which there have been a disproportionate number of judgement summonses can scarcely be faulted – nobody is obliged to offer their goods on a universal basis. But to refuse to supply credit (or goods selling on credit) to an applicant on the grounds he/she lives in a high risk area must seem like unfair discrimination, and is probably illegal under the Consumer Credit Act. And this could be the result of using Mosaic, whose area classifications are based, in part, on such data. CCN's interpretation (following OFT advice) is that Mosaic classifications can be used to select prospects, with perfect propriety; they can only be used for credit screening in conjunction with other appropriate criteria (e.g. data from the applicant's form of application).

Mention of unfair discrimination prompts another thought: CCN have deliberately excluded from Mosaic all census variables dealing with racial origin; they are alone in this.

CCN initially chose 300 census variables from among the 4,000 available, and tested various combinations of these before arriving at a list of 38. This is the smallest number of census variables used by any of these systems; CCN stress the need to use only variables that have a high level of penetration among a large number of EDs.

Mosaic, then, uses 38 census variables, taken from EDs and ascribed to postcodes. It also aggregates at postcode level 16 other variables; these non-census items need some further consideration. Some information is gathered from the electoral register, which is inspected annually; other items come from the Lord Chancellor's list. Finally there is one source of information not available to CCN's competitors – the record of credit references sought by finance houses, credit card companies, and retail stores for whom CCN has acted as a credit reference agency.

We have seen that one of the problems with the census data is the way in which it ages. Mosaic attempts to deal with this problem by ascribing to the variables that go into its cluster analysis different weights. So, although the census data accounts for 38 out of 54 variables used, the overall weight ascribed to it in the clustering process is no more than 46%, the remaining 16 variables being collectively weighted at 54%. (Strictly speaking the electoral register weighting ought to be altered downwards each year, but CCN do not yet appear to be doing this; the interesting thing about the system is that it would be possible.) None of the non-census data is more than two years old at any time.

These 54 weighted variables are then used in a cluster analysis to cluster the 130,000 postcode areas into 58 Mosaic types, which in turn aggregate into 10 groups. It is noteworthy that the Mosaic types include a number of clusters identified as "Post-1981 housing" – an identification made from the Post Office's Postal Address File (PAF); systems whose clusters are based on EDs cannot make this distinction. It is also interesting that many postcodes that are in the same ED fall into different Mosaic clusters: this ought to be an index of the extra discriminatory power of the non-census variables used by Mosaic. Of course, these non-census variables, and the weightings ascribed to them, will not necessarily be of equal relevance to all potential users.

The services offered by CCN in connection with Mosaic are:

i) *Postcoding* CCN, like Pinpoint, is a Post Office approved supplier of computerized postcoding services; it can postcode client lists and obtain financial assistance for the client from the Post Office.

ii) *Prospect profiling and scoring* The systems that Mosaic offers for these purposes are not in principle different from those of their competitors. Any differences in practice will arise from the different construction of the demographic classification itself.

iii) *Mosaic coding* As with other systems, Mosaic codes can be added to client files under the terms of a leasing agreement for the Mosaic directory. The initial coding work can be done at the same time as postcoding the file, if that function is also required.

iv) *Market monitor* This is a regular monthly service offered by CCN to clients with customer accounts. Each month the client sends in a tape of his/her accounts; CCN analyses these, by Mosaic type, and by a variety of geographic factors, and produces both a set of printed reports and a floppy disk. This disk can be used by the client on his/her own micro to produce, on screen or on paper, area maps of the data reported on.

v) *CAIS* This stands for Credit Account Information Sharing. Some 60 mail order/retail/finance house clients of CCN provide a monthly tape of their account customers, and the performance of each; this information goes into a database where it is available only to other members of the club; the information can of course be profiled by Mosaic.

vi) *Credit applications* CCN vets applications for credit on behalf of clients against an electoral register database overlaid with the Lord Chancellor's list – and with details of other credit applications. The more clients use this system, the more powerful it becomes, and the fact of a credit application by an individual is itself a piece of data fed to the Mosaic classification of the area concerned, which, to complete the circle, is a factor in reviewing the application.

vii) *Nationwide consumer file* This is our old friend the electoral register, held by CCN and updated annually. It is also overlaid with a regular record of new postal addresses from the PAF; it can be profiled by Mosaic, analysed by TV or ILR areas and by all the familiar geographic breakdowns.

**j) Superprofiles**  This product belongs to Credit & Data Marketing Services Ltd., a subsidiary of Littlewoods, who bought it in 1987 from its original designers at O.E.McIntyre. This is the newest of the systems considered here, having been launched in 1986. It is also almost certainly the system which has benefited from the greatest quantity of academic research and testing – using facilities and staff at Newcastle and Liverpool Universities – to establish the optimal structure of census variables and ED clusters.

Initial selection of census variables was based on testing a wide variety of candidates against Littlewoods trading data, to see which were the best discriminators. This resulted in the selection of 55 variables (in fact not very different in numbers or composition from those used by other systems). The next step was to cluster the 130,000 EDs using these 55 variables. Every fifth number between 5 and 1,000 clusters was tried, to give the best compromise (although that implies a degree of subjective judgement) between concision and precision. Finally, the number of 150 clusters was chosen. This is more than double the number of clusters used by any other system; if matters had been left there, the result would have to appear unwieldy.

The next step consisted in ranking the 150 clusters (now simply identified by a number from 1-150) on the basis of 10 further census variables not included in the original clustering. This ranking was intended to give an initial indication of wealth. Then a further 25 geographic variables (indicating region and broad employment type) were added for each ED and aggregated at a cluster level. These do not affect the already-determined clustering, but are used at the next stage. Finally, market performance data derived from TGI was applied to the clusters in order to group them into 10 Lifestyles and 36 Target Markets. The Target Markets are ranked from 1-36 in order of affluence, and it is interesting that this measure of affluence, derived from TGI data, is different from, while clearly still related to, the wealth ranking of clusters derived from census data. 36 Target Markets is a much more manageable number, and more closely related to the number of clusters used in other systems. But the important point to note is that the grouping of clusters into target markets was accomplished by use of current performance data: it is the intention of CDMS to repeat this exercise with new data annually (the first grouping was done in January 1987). This means that, although the basic census data cannot change till 1993 – and the geographic data will not change anyway in the short to medium term – and although the clusters based on that census data cannot change, yet the Target Market and Lifestyle groupings can change annually. This is the CDMS answer to the problem of ageing census data –

different from that of Mosaic, but a movement in the same direction.
The services offered by CDMS in relation to Superprofiles are:

i)  *Directory licences*    The Superprofile directory can be leased
    for a minimum period of three years at an annual charge
    varying from £3,100 to £12,050 depending on the size of the
    client's file. Payments fall by 50% after the first three years.
    After signing a lease, the client can apply Superprofile codes
    to his/her own list.

ii) *Rollcall*    This is the name given to CDMS electoral register
    service, which offers essentially the same facilities as its
    competitors.

iii) *Tailor-made clusters*    CDMS will design a clustering system
     of anywhere between 5 and 1,000 ED clusters (based on the
     55 original census variables) to suit the particular needs of
     an individual client.

iv) *Statsfile*    This is a system for performing customer pene-
    tration analysis. It will take data on client customers, and
    produce penetration reports by Superprofile cluster, Target
    Markets, and Lifestyles, or by any of the standard geographic
    expressions. The interesting aspect of this system is that it
    can be run, under licence, on the client's own micro; a floppy
    disk contains the Statsfile system, and there is a package to
    convert the client's data, as held on a mainframe, into input
    for a micro. This does in principle enable client marketing
    staff to use data much more creatively than is possible where
    every question has to be structured for answer at a remote
    bureau. The cost of a Statsfile licence is £5,000p.a. CDMS
    offer relatively cheap facilities to test the viability of Statsfile
    before signing an agreement.

v)  *Profiling etc.*    CDMS offer the usual facilities for profiling
    client files, scoring, selection, retail site assessment, etc.

**k) Conclusions**    Ultimately there are only two questions that a marketing person wants to ask about such systems. Do all or any of
them work, in the sense of assisting more profitable targeting of
marketing effort? And which one is the best?

The principle behind all these systems – that demographics, as
expressed in census data, can tell us something useful about markets

– is undoubtedly sound. All of them have achieved profitable results for a number of clients. The systems are all better at locating areas of poverty than of affluence; they are all better at relatively broad-brush descriptions of geographic areas (of a kind that can be invaluable to the retail trade) than at picking out individual persons for direct mail approaches (the purpose, ironically, for which they were designed). However, even at an individual level, they are all capable of providing a deeper insight into the demands of the market-place.

There can be no question of selecting a "best buy" since the needs of every user are necessarily different. But I will venture some tentative generalizations. Acorn is much the oldest-established system, and CACI as a company has the longest experience – although some of their competitors now have ex-CACI staff. Acorn is still the best-known and understood, and most widely-used system; if compatibility with what other parties are doing, or with their terminology, is a factor, one should seriously consider going no further. However, since the development of the original concept, CACI has not been the most innovative in this field.

Pinpoint has followed largely in Acorn's steps. It has done a service to the industry in pointing out some earlier sloppy habits that no one else wanted to know about, but it is doubtful if this has enabled it to retain any competitive advantage. Its strength lies in two areas: anyone that sees significant advantage in a sophisticated mapping service should certainly explore Pinpoint's facilities; and the development of Finpin (to which there may be sister services added) does look impressive for those selling financial services. Neither CACI nor Pinpoint has addressed the problem of systems deterioration as the census data ages; Mosaic and Superprofiles have.

CCN would have to be a first stop for anyone with credit reference or associated problems – not just because the system is fundamentally good, but because of the volume of data supporting it. And Mosaic, also underpinned by that volume of data supplementing the census information, has a broader basis of static data than any of its competitors. It is also the only system which can claim to be, without extra effort, improving rather than deteriorating over time, by virtue of constantly added data.

Superprofiles' approach to the ageing problem is extremely ingenious, but I doubt if it is as good an answer as Mosaic's. Moreover, the large number of its clusters, and their smaller sizes, may make it particularly vulnerable to demographic changes. On the other hand, the weight of academic experience that has gone into this system is impressive, and the facility to run analysis systems on the client's own micro is a real breakthrough.

## 3  Psychographic Data

Whereas the use of demographic data in marketing has been growing in the UK ever since its introduction in the mid 1970s (and in the USA somewhat earlier), the use of psychographic, or life style, data – at least in the sense of having such information available in the market-place – is a new phenomenon in this country, which made its first tentative appearance in 1983, and is only now getting under way, largely following in American footsteps.

The claim advanced by those who wish to sell a psychographic service to marketers is that very substantial numbers of people can be persuaded to provide comprehensive information about themselves, their households, their possessions, behaviour, and interests; further, that this data can be made to serve two purposes:

i) It can provide, for any given trader, specific information about the kinds of people who buy his products, enabling him to tailor his advertising approach according to their characteristics.

ii) It can provide generalized information about a very large market-place, making possible extremely precise targeting of prospects based on self-submitted individual characteristics.

Our purpose here is to examine the present status of psychographic systems; to indicate what systems are on offer from whom; to discuss the similarities and differences of competing systems, and to give some evaluation of the claims made for the methodology as a marketing tool.

**a) Demographics versus psychographics**   As we have seen, the use of demographic data was pioneered by the direct mail industry in the 1970s, with the object of finding a way to segment such huge, but undifferentiated, lists as the electoral register. But the only demographic data universally available (the census data) relates not to the individual persons, or households, that are the direct marketer's target, but to groups of households of an only roughly homogeneous kind. Moreover, the census data is an aggregated snapshot of the population at an increasingly remote point in time. For these reasons, demographics in direct marketing terms have had only a limited success; their true value probably lies in the geographic analysis of population groups for marketers whose prime interest is in groups rather than individuals – such as retailers.

Psychographics, by contrast, looks as though it may possess the capacity to revolutionize the direct marketing industry, and direct mail in particular, turning it belatedly, but for real, into that which it has always claimed to be – a highly selective and carefully targeted medium of communication between seller and buyer. Ironically, the techniques involved were not developed in the first instance either by or for the existing direct mail industry, but for manufacturers of consumer goods who were increasingly finding the conventional advertising and market research media either inadequate, or poor value for money.

The use of demographics and psychographics illustrates, better than anything else, the current convergence of marketing techniques. Each has something to offer to a variety of users, who would historically have regarded themselves as belonging to very different disciplines. Psychographics – that is to say the building and use of databases consisting of information about individual consumers' life styles – has a contribution to make in each of the three classic areas of marketing:

Market Research
Advertising
Selling

After a brief consideration of the general methodology of psychographic services, we will look at each of these areas.

**b) Methodology**   There were originally three sets of psychographic offerings in the UK market-place. Two now remain, both at quite an early stage of development. The original three were:

DataBank, originally established by ConsumerQuest and later marketed by The List Shop. This company still owns DataBank, but is no longer trading. No new names have been added to this database since 1987; residual marketing of what is now an elderly, and declining, list is in the hands of Cheryl Nathan List Broking.

Behaviourbank, the property of Computer Marketing Technologies (CMT).

The Lifestyle Selector, owned, operated and marketed by National Demographics and Lifestyles (NDL).

All three operations collect(ed), by means of questionnaires distributed to consumer households, a wide range of information about individual consumers, which is then stored on a database. The method of distributing questionnaires varies from one company to another – and this is likely to be significant for particular users. All three operate a system whereby particular questions in the survey – or, in one case, the entire questionnaire – can be sponsored by individual companies. The returned questionnaires will be handled by the operating company, and the information on each will be data-captured. Sponsoring companies will receive full reports on the survey results in a pre-agreed format. Certain information (for example anything that is brand-specific) will be regarded as confidential to the sponsoring company, which may, in addition, have certain continuing rights in further use of the data. Other data, including names and addresses, will become part of the general database, which may be used to provide names on a highly selective basis for direct mail users. Other, more sophisticated uses are in principle obtainable, and will without doubt become available as the market learns how to demand them; at the moment this particular market-place is still rudimentary.

From the point of view of the companies operating these services, this methodology is highly satisfactory: Companies A, B, and C each pay a fee to cover the distribution of questions, and related services; as a by-product the operating company obtains voluminous information which can be sold – again with added-value services – to other clients X, Y, and Z. What the client can obtain, we will now consider.

**c) Market Research** The manufacturers of consumer goods who want to discover more about the nature of the end-users of their products – perhaps in order to determine whether their choice (or their agency's choice) of advertising media is optimal – face a problem: almost certainly they have no record of who these end-users are, and no established means of communication with them. Gradually this situation is changing: it is now common form for motor manufacturers, for instance, to obtain from their dealers the names and addresses of customers, together with basic details of each purchase, which can be built into a database, enabling the manufacturers to communicate with their customers directly, rather than through blanket advertising media. Such a database, however, is unlikely to contain significant information about individual life styles, or to be of much value from a market research point of view.

The traditional solution to this problem is therefore to commission a market research company to undertake a survey. The value of even the most basic database, in this context, is that it provides a sampling universe for the market researcher. With or without this assistance, he or she will then, probably in a series of face-to-face interviews, record the life styles of a sample of buyers, extrapolate to cover the universe, and note the differences in his or her findings from what is known about the population at large.

The problem with conventional market research is three-fold. First, even at a modest level – the minimum required for the desired degree of statistical significance – it is expensive; extended to any substantial scale it becomes extremely expensive, with costs being closely related to numbers of persons surveyed. Second, the statistical tabulations produced from this kind of research are its sole output: the rules of the Market Research Society positively forbid the attribution of names to research data. Third, the methodology is somewhat inflexible, and requires 20/20 vision at the time of designing the questionnaire: it really isn't practicable to look at the response, and discover, at that point, some interesting further question that one would like to explore with certain respondents.

The strengths of the psychographic approach are the reverse of these weaknesses. First, the methodology is cheap: the design, printing and distribution of questionnaires, the data-capture of responses, and the analysis of results, should give a cost measured in pence per respondent. Second, the chief by-product of the whole process is a potentially valuable list of self-submitted names and addresses, with a wide range of information about each. Third, because this list of names is available, any kind of follow-up suggested by the results of the original questionnaire is simple.

But there is one major drawback. The essence of conventional market research lies in obtaining response from a representative sample of the universe that one is trying to profile. Thus, one might go to a representative sample of the total population in order to discover what proportion of UK adults regularly drive a motor car; one would pick a representative sample of Porsche buyers in order to determine the age breakdown of all Porsche buyers. And so on. The trouble with life-style databases is that they seldom – never in the case of the systems examined in this paper – constitute a representative sample of anything definable; it is therefore not possible to extrapolate from what a life-style study shows to a universal statement. The very fact that the information on a life-style database is volunteered by the persons to whom it refers – an enormous strength in a direct marketing context – means that it contains a self-selected, and therefore non-representative, sample.

Tony Coad, Managing Director of NDL, tells the story of a US company selling portable barbecue sets; they directed their advertising at outdoor types liable to take off on hunting expeditions – until a life-style survey of their buyers suggested that their product appeal was dominantly to yuppies in metropolitan apartment blocks, on

whose verandahs the barbecues fitted conveniently. A nice illustration; what we are not told – because nobody knows – is the precise
proportion of barbecue buyers that fitted either profile. And nobody
knows because the individuals surveyed were not a representative
sample of all buyers.

Of course, this may not matter greatly: it is perfectly possible to
obtain a worthwhile insight into one's market without having to
quantify it to three places of decimals. We are, after all, in business
to record profits, not statistics. And the larger the proportion that
our sample forms of the total, the less its technically non-representative nature will matter. So, if we have access to a life-style database
on which are recorded 30% of this year's customers for a given item,
we will give more credence to what such a source appears to tell us
about our market than we would if the same records constituted
only 3% of the total. It is important to recognize the theoretical
limitations of what this kind of data can tell us; it is not necessarily
important to invoke the last degree of precision for our calculations.

Finally, conventional market research and research via a life-style
database are not necessarily competitive approaches. One of the
hardest problems in market research is knowing before the event
what questions one wants to ask. Because the life-style questionnaire
is a cheap way of obtaining large quantities of data, it may make
sense to use it as a sort of saturation coverage, from the results of
which one can construct a small-scale, more precise piece of conventional research. Such an approach will both make it easier to frame
one's ultimate questions better, and to economize on overall research
costs.

**d) Advertising** The advertising function can make use of a life-style
database in three main ways. First, as we have seen while discussing
market research, it is possible to create a profile of the responding
customers on such a database in order to determine whether existing
advertising policy is consistent with what the life-style information
reveals. Second, one can use a life-style database to select groups
of individuals to whom to address a direct advertising message considered appropriate to their presumed needs or interests. Thirdly,
one can vary the terms in which that message is presented to suit
the particular circumstances of individual members of the selected
groups.

**e) Selling** The use of life-style databases in selling implies, of
course, selling by direct mail. Direct mail has always claimed to be
the medium, par excellence, which enables the user to target sales
efforts to specific individuals more likely than the undifferentiated

mass to be interested in his/her offer. In the context of a user who
has for years past been cultivating a database of his/her own customers, with records of their purchases, payment methods, changes of
address, and so on, this claim has merit. Just as it is highly questionable whether demographic information can do very much to enhance
the responsiveness of a database that already contains substantial
purchase information, so it must also be doubted whether life-style
information about customers' possessions, habits, and tastes can
effect great improvements in a system already acquainted with their
purchases. But where a sales effort is being directed not at past
customers for whom considerable histories exist, but at cold prospects, acquired from the electoral register, or from a list broker, the
situation is altogether different. Such campaigns are no more
"targeted" than a direct response advertisement in a national newspaper – perhaps less so. Segmenting the potential mass audience by
reference to demographic characteristics – a practice that has become
widespread over the last ten years – can certainly help, but to a
rather limited extent. But to be able to select prospects from a
database of persons known to have responded to a questionnaire
through the mail, and known to be willing to receive advertising
material by post; to be able furthermore to segment this audience
by reference to its self-submitted characteristics – that is an altogether
different matter, going a very long way to justify the contention that
direct mail is a precise instrument.

What is needed now in the life style, or psychographic, field, is
the same level of professional expertise in modelling, scoring, regression analysis and such techniques, as already exists in large users of
established customer lists (such as the Consumers' Association, or
Reader's Digest) and, indeed, in the companies offering demographic
services. It is ironic that the most sophisticated statistical techniques
should be daily used to provide demographically profiled selections
from the electoral register – rather akin to using solid gold cutlery
to eat chip butties – while the chief demand to date on psychographic
databases has been for lists of households with gardens, or of people
with an interest in DIY – analogous to drinking Gevrey Chambertin
out of polystyrene cups.

There is no problem for companies in the psychographic field in
acquiring such skills: in some cases they are already in place. So far
the demand for their exercise has been slow to surface. No doubt
this will change quite quickly.

**f) Critical mass** Part of the reason for this present lack of sophistication lies in the relatively small size of the life-style databases
now available. Although the quantity of information available on

any one name is large, and thus very complex selections are possible, this may not make too much sense on a list of, say, 250,000 households. This raises the whole question of what size might ultimately be achieved by such a database.

If we regard the useful life of a single, non-updated, database entry as being between two and three years, then the answer to this question is going to depend on the number of questionnaires that a company can distribute in this period, and on the response rate that it can expect. This in turn will be affected by the different methods of distribution used by current practitioners, and on the incentives offered to consumers to respond. As we shall see, different practitioners have different expectations. My own view would be that a lifestyle database of less than 2 million households (which is close to 10% of the UK population) is not likely to be viable long-term. On the other hand there seems little reason to suppose that a database of at least this size cannot be created and sustained without undue effort.

**g) DataBank**  DataBank was the property of ConsumerQuest, a company set up in 1983 to operate in what was then the virgin field, in the UK, of psychographic, or life style, marketing. Questionnaires were sent out under the ConsumerQuest name, and in 1985 names were offered from the database thus compiled. ConsumerQuest itself is no longer trading; the understanding in the trade is that it ran out of money in early 1987, and its erstwhile directors have departed hither and yon.

The original ConsumerQuest questionnaire was distributed mainly through the Home Delivery Service (HDS) of the Post Office – i.e. an unaddressed blanket coverage of specific areas. Acorn classifications of the electoral register were used to exclude the areas of greatest poverty which were thought to be of least interest. Response to the questionnaire varied from 1% (in a number of urban areas) to 6% (in some rural areas), giving a total database, compiled in 1985-6, of some 250,000 households, or 320,000 names. The questions covered in the questionnaire related to:

Household composition
Age
Occupation
Motoring Habits
Travel
Hobbies
Financial Affairs

ConsumerQuest's early version of the questionnaire attracted a certain amount of public criticism for seeming to be other than what it was; this was quickly rectified, and those completing the questionnaire were also asked to indicate whether or not they were willing to receive direct mail advertising for items that matched their expressed interests.

ConsumerQuest offered entry to a free prize draw as an incentive for filling in the questionnaire – although this was presented in a fairly low-key manner. Responses to the questionnaire were returned through the mail.

With the exception of one question on motor cars, none of the questions asked were brand-specific; however, individual companies were invited to sponsor, exclusively or on a shared basis, individual questions. They then received exclusive (or shared) rights for 90 days in the results of these questions for direct mail purposes. Not all of the information collected on the questionnaire forms was retained in the database. The reason given was that some of this information is short-term by definition – e.g. the answer to the question "If you were thinking of buying a new vehicle within the next six months, which brand would you consider?" For this reason, the answers to a number a questions are concatenated: Cheryl Nathan List Broking has a full list of the data available on the database.

DataBank is now almost entirely of historical interest; the list is not being refreshed by new surveys, and usage is small. Most of what the company set out to do, and some of the staff who set out to do it, now rest with Behaviourbank.

**h) Behaviourbank**   This is the name of a psychographic database owned by Computer Marketing Technologies (CMT). This company was set up in the USA in 1980, and has been conducting questionnaire surveys there under the name Select & Save. The company is represented in this country by CMT (UK), which handles the data relating to fmcg products, and Bricoda, which deals with the non-fmcg side of the business, with list rentals, and with the issuing of surveys, similar to the DataBank survey, under the banner of the National Shoppers' Survey.

Behaviourbank's effort is directed mostly at fmcg companies. The aim is to find sponsors for the questions to be included in a questionnaire which will be distributed over a 6-month period. At the end of that time the questionnaire – and possibly the sponsors – will change. The sponsor will receive full statistical reports, both on his sponsored question and on the non-branded life style questions; he will also qualify for three free uses of the names of responders to this questionnaire; thereafter further use will be at the reduced rate of £40/thousand. He will pay £250 per question sponsored, per thousand questionnaires distributed, with a minimum order value of £150,000; this covers printing and distribution of questionnaires, data-capture of response, statistical analysis, printing of reports.

Information collected by Behaviourbank covers:

| | |
|---|---|
| Credit Cards | Home Ownership |
| Travel | Type of House |
| Investments/Insurance | Length of Occupancy |
| Health Interests | Marital Status |
| Sports Interests | Adult & Child Ages |
| Outdoors Interests | Grandchildren |
| Social/Charity Interests | Income |
| Collecting Interests | Occupation |
| Food/Wine Interests | Working Women |
| Electrical Products | Cars |

The incentive for the consumer to fill in the questionnaire is the promise of a free pack of discount vouchers on branded groceries and household goods; these are personalized, laser-printed, and despatched as part of the response fulfilment process. However, the manufacturers whose coupons are included in the packs to be despatched can call for the value of each coupon, and the message on it, to be varied according to the nature of the answers given in the questionnaire. Behaviourbank also sells space in the fulfilment envelope for further brochures etc.; these too can be included or omitted on the basis of response. In this way, manufacturers can distribute their coupons much more precisely than is possible at point of sale – concentrating on the buyers of competing brands in order to persuade them to switch, rather than on their own established customers. Moreover, the activity in this field of any one manufacturer is invisible – or at the least unquantifiable – to the competitors. It is alleged that the redemption rate of coupons distributed in this way is 20 times higher (30-50%) than the norm for point-of-sale coupons. (N.B. Fulfilment costs are not included in the charges quoted above, and will vary according to volume of printing and complexity.)

Methods of distribution for the questionnaire vary; some household delivery is done, but the bulk is via loose inserts in magazines and newspapers. Claimed response rate in the USA is 10% (the American database has 7 million names); reliable rates are not yet available for this country, but the first pilot questionnaire, in early 1987, pulled 13%. The UK database now comprises 1½ million households, or 2.9 million consumers ; this is forecast to rise to 3-4 million by mid-1990.

Data-capture is performed overseas (in Jamaica and Sri Lanka). Business names are rented at £70 per thousand, and others at £60, plus, in each case, £5-7 for selections.

**j) The Lifestyle selector**   This is the name given by NDL International Ltd. to its database. NDL – or National Demographics & Lifestyles Inc. – originated in the USA. NDL in this country is an affiliate of the American company, and has substantial offices and staff in central London. Its approach is significantly different, both in objective and in methodology, from that of the other two players examined above.

NDL designs a separate questionnaire for each manufacturer-client. The client thus "sponsors" an entire questionnaire, and this is distributed by being included in his packed products at point of manufacture. It follows that NDL's initial target clients tend to be manufacturers of consumer durables. The clients pay a flat-rate fee of £6,000. For this, NDL will help them to design a questionnaire (which the clients will produce and insert in packs at their own cost), data-capture the response, analyse and report on the results, and hand over a tape of names and addresses with product-specific data. This agreement lasts for one year; reports are provided on the first 4,000 responses, plus 3 further quarterly reports. Thereafter the agreement can be continued annually for a further £6,000 p.a.; the sum is independent of the number of questionnaires distributed.

Although questionnaires are individually-tailored, the normal format consists of questions covering such subjects as:

| | |
|---|---|
| Date of Purchase | Sex |
| Product | Date of Birth |
| Price | Marital Status |
| Place Purchased | Occupation |
| Reason for Purchase | Ages of Children |
| Source of Information | Family Income |
| Important Product Qualities | Credit Cards |
| Use of Product | Housing |
| Related Product Interests/ Activities | Car |

Product-specific data from these questionnaires belongs solely to the client; non-specific data belongs to NDL, and is included on the database. Names from this database are available for rental, and the company stresses that *any* combination of selections is acceptable to the system.

At the time of writing NDL has 67 clients in the UK. Response rates are reported as being even higher than in the USA, averaging 20-25%, but with some running as high as 50%. However, NDL has insisted from the start that every questionnaire must contain a clear opportunity for the consumer to indicate that he or she does NOT wish to receive promotion; the company claims that 30% of responders avail themselves of this opportunity. (The company's whole mode of operation has come under intense scrutiny from the Data Protection Registrar in 1988; its current procedures would appear to have satisfied this severe critic.) This clearly reduces the net response rate, so far as further use of the names is concerned – but it also does indicate that those net names are genuinely prepared to receive further promotion material. During late 1988, responses from all current efforts were coming in at the rate of 35,000 per week, and the database had reached some 1.6 million names, the ultimate aim being 8 million households. Records are discarded after two years if no further movement takes place.

NDL also offers to rent to its clients PCs complete with software and disks to enable them to run their own product-related data – at a cost of £5,000p.a. plus £1,000 per PC. NDL's data-capture is performed in Barbados; it uses the mainframe of the American company in Denver for its database, but also has a substantial computer installation in London.

NDL's publicity literature makes much more reference than does that of its competitors to the possibilities of sophisticated customer targeting that such a database makes possible, instead of thinking in terms of discrete "lists". The company does possess the skilled staff to implement advanced schemes of profiling, modelling, and scoring for customers, and if the database grows to even half the size projected, such facilities will be of great value. A client who has used an NDL questionnaire will then be able to build a profile of his own customers from the responses, and to select from the other names on the database those that match this profile to a given degree of accuracy.

**k) Conclusion** Psychographic, or life-style, marketing is still in its infancy in this country; it is fairly new in the United States as well, but has there accomplished enough to demonstrate its real potential. What has been done in the UK so far does at least suggest that there is every indication the UK market is at least as responsive to the concept as is the US market.

The first indigenous attempt in the UK, undertaken by Consumer-Quest, does not appear to have flourished. Although a small database was created, the company lost its opportunity to carve out a position for itself ahead of the competition (as, for instance, Acorn did in the demographic field).

The two remaining contenders – although they are not in very direct competition – are both drawing on American resources in terms of experience. Behaviourbank has headed straight for a particular niche in the market, trying to muscle in on the coupon incentive business and offering a powerful new weapon to fmcg brand managers – at least until everyone is using their methodology and we are all back at square one. Meanwhile, this does look like an exciting new tool. Whether the database that will result from this activity will have predictive power for the general user is perhaps less certain: I would expect its profile to be somewhat down-market.

The List Selector has much the most elegant solution for distributing questionnaires. Moreover, the chosen method of distribution will tend to create a relatively up-market result. I do not believe it probable that any life style list can be made, in the UK, to grow to a size of 8 million households, but even a third of that (which I do believe can be exceeded within the two-year useful lifespan of a name) would make a superb database – *provided that* adequate customer education is available in the arts of name selection and multi-variate analysis.

It has seemed worth while to deal at some length with specialized demographic and psychographic systems, partly because, while widely talked about, they, and the differences between the various systems on offer, are not well understood, and partly because they do illustrate a number of interesting facets of the database problem, namely:

a) how to apply publicly-available census data to individual records of customers or prospects, based on their geographic locations;

b) how to acquire, or deduce, a limited amount of information about individual households from publicly-available records such as the electoral register, or the Lord Chancellor's list of county court judgements, etc.;

c) how to obtain personal, or life-style, information from at least a proportion of one's potential audience by questionnaire;

d) in general, how to convert a mere list of names and addresses into something more valuable.

But we should end this section by coming back to where we started the whole chapter – with the collection of sales-related customer data. Demographic and psychographic data can make a welcome additional slab of information for a customer database; equally, when we are looking at prospects rather than customers, and therefore necessarily at people about whom we have very little information to begin with, then the acquisition of demographic and psychographic data can make a very great difference to the value of our database. But far and away the most important and valuable information any trader has about any consumers is information about his own company's dealings with them. It is towards the capture of that information above all that every effort should first be devoted; when that has been done, and a strategy has been worked out, and proved in practice, for the use of that data, then the bells and whistles that extraneous information represents can be added at leisure.

## 4 Business-related Data

It is a perennial problem in discussing databases – or direct marketing – that we must consider two groups of users of the techniques in question: those whose marketing effort is directed towards consumers, and those who are addressing themselves primarily to other business people. Chapter 3 on Database Applications used examples from both camps. In this chapter, some of what we have had to say so far has had greater relevance to consumer than to business marketing; some has had little or no point for the latter category, and in some places considerations relevant to business marketing have been left out altogether. We will try in this short section to fill in some of the gaps.

**a) Privacy** Those whose databases hold information primarily on business customers rather than private persons are not necessarily exempt thereby from the Data Protection Act – although by no means all the possible issues are totally clear. If, for example, one holds on a computer the name and address of Marks and Spencer plc, together with details of that company's dealings with one's own business, then, even though in other contexts Marks and Spencer plc is a legal person, this information is not personal data within the meaning of the Act – which is concerned solely with living individuals. The same position would probably apply even if Mr Marks and Mr Spencer were both alive and conducting the affairs of their emporia – since the entity "Marks and Spencer plc" is distinct from Messrs Marks and Spencer either singly or jointly. If, however, your data about Marks and Spencer includes the information that Lord Sieff is its Chairman, then it would appear incontrovertible that this is personal data, within the meaning of the Act, about Lord Sieff.

Again, if your database held the information that Robin Fairlie, an unincorporated individual, was running a business from 15 Vincent Terrace, London N1 8HJ (whether or not that was also his private address) it would be difficult to maintain that this was other than personal data. As always with the Data Protection Act, the answer has to be: if in any kind of doubt, register. It can do no harm; the cost is marginal, and probably less than scrubbing around trying to find an exemption or other way out.

**b) Duplication**  Everything said above under this heading applies to business addresses as it does to consumer addresses. But the problems in the former case go further. First, business addresses are typically longer and more cumbersome than consumer addresses:

John Smith Esq.,
Managing Director,
J. Bloggs & Co. Ltd.,
Bloggspalace,
George Orwell Industrial Estate,
Wigan Pier,
WIGAN,
Lancs. WI17 2FA

gives a not uncommon flavour. Such addresses represent a real challenge to computer programs to analyse, to verify against the PAF, to correct where necessary, and to postcode where this has not been done. Lots of bureaux in the market-place today are offering postcoding and address correction facilities. Almost all of them will admit, when pressed, that these computerized facilities operate much less effectively for business than for consumer addresses. This problem is dealt with more fully in Chapter 5 below, section 4 – Postage.

Second, the owners of business databases must address, and answer, a fundamental question about the data they hold: are they primarily interested in the individual persons in their database, or in the holders of particular job-titles, or simply in targeting particular companies, or indeed trades. This will influence their attitude towards updating their information. Updating a business database poses more numerous, and more difficult, problems than are usually encountered with a consumer database: these will be discussed further in the next chapter, section 1 b.

**c) Demographic and psychographic data**  In some cases census-derived demographic data will be very important to a business database. Where, for example, the records on the database relate to retail shops, then the demographic profile of the surrounding area is highly relevant. Indeed, in such a case one may well – depending on the nature of the shops concerned – wish to amalgamate census data from a number of enumeration districts within a given radius, to give an overall profile of an outlet's market-place. *Individual* demographic or psychographic data will also be valuable in such cases, when it can be expressed in statistical form: e.g. that of the 1,763 persons for whom we have information in such and such an area, 35% have expressed a burning interest in archery. Data manipulations of this kind are the bread and butter of the types of database bureaux we have discussed above.

# 5 Data Handling

Collecting information for a database is one thing; keeping it up to date is altogether another. It will not have escaped the notice of anyone reading the provisions of the Data Protection Act in the previous chapter, that the fifth principle in the Act provides that personal data should be kept up to date. To the harassed businessman, who desires nothing more than to keep *all* his data up to date, but is frequently puzzled how to find appropriate means towards this end, it may seem that an Act of Parliament is a curious place to find such a pious statement of the obvious. Act or no Act, it is an inescapable fact that personal data loses accuracy over time – indeed minute by minute, thus following the universal law of entropy, that everything decays. So there is no point in setting out to build a database unless thought has first been given to how it is to be maintained and updated.

The first thing that anyone renting a list of names and addresses, with or without associated information, should seek to know is: when was the data collected, and what is done, with what periodicity, to maintain it in an accurate condition. Of course, some of the information on a database is not subject to updating, or change, in this way: once-for-all information about historical fact, if properly verified at time of collection, will scarcely require updating. Which is why a database will never record, directly, a person's age, but always their date of birth. Similarly with product purchases, or other events that happen at a moment in time – if true once, they continue to be true. Data, however, about a continuing state of affairs rather than a precise occurrence is another matter, and nowhere can this be more clearly illustrated than in reference to the name and address itself. We will consider the problems separately for consumer and business addresses.

**a) Consumer**   Approximately 12% of the population moves house every year. Or, to put it another way, the average person moves home once in every eight years. This gives a simple indication of the speed with which a consumer database, if not properly maintained, goes out of date in respect of its most fundamental piece of data, without which the rest is of questionable value – who lives where. If one rents a list of names and addresses that has been compiled over a five-year period, one knows (or should know) that something like 60% of the persons on the oldest part of the list no longer live at the address on record – unless there has been a regular process of maintenance to offset this factor.

List maintenance takes a variety of forms, and some of these are more valuable than others. A publisher, for example, whose database is composed of subscribers to one or more learned periodicals, may reasonably feel that his customers will do much of his list maintenance work for him. He will be well-advised to print a reminder on the backs of his magazine wrappers for subscribers to fill in and return if they are about to move, or have just moved. But mostly his data subjects will *wish* to hear regularly from him with the periodicals for which they have paid, and can therefore be trusted to notify changes of address fairly quickly. This in turn means that any user who rents a list of periodical subscribers has reasonable security (depending to some extent on the frequency of publication) that the addresses concerned will not be too wildly astray: there is a built-in feedback mechanism.

People who are members of a club, or similar organization, are less reliable. By and large they are not obtaining a perceived benefit *through the mail* from the organization to which they belong (and even if the organization produces a periodical, this is probably not the subscriber's prime interest in joining). Such people have, therefore rather less incentive to notify the organization of a move – at least until the time comes to renew their subscriptions. The addresses on such club databases are therefore about as good as their last renewal dates: if renewal is annual, and individual renewals are spread randomly through the year, then one could reasonably expect anything up to 6% of addresses to be invalid at any one time – but not more.

Lists of past buyers, or guarantee card holders, or enquirers, occupy an even shadier area. In some cases there may have been no occasion for communication to or from the individuals concerned since their names were collected – in which case the list becomes pretty valueless after a couple of years at the outside. But it may be that these past buyers have been mailed regularly with further offers, or information. Those that have responded – depending on recency of response – are clearly more likely to be still contactable.

But a database which is being mailed regularly benefits not only from being able to update the addresses of respondents; it is also the case that a proportion of those mailing pieces that fail to reach their addressees will be returned marked "Gone Away": this is, of course , a valuable piece of information, since even though one may not know where the addressee has gone to, at least one knows not to expect him or her at the old address, and one can avoid the cost of uselessly writing to him or her there.

The issue of "gone aways" is more complex than it might at first appear. There are a number of points worth making:

i) Every mailing piece addressed from a permanent list or database should carry a return address on the reverse, so that rejected mail can be returned easily;

ii) All "gone aways" should be recorded on the database;

iii) List owners who are renting their lists to third parties should be prepared to pay the renter a small sum for each "gone away" returned to them: not only does this recompense the renter for some of the money that has been wasted, it also assists the owner in keeping a list clean *and* improves the credibility of the list in the eyes of the next prospective renter.

iv) However, not all mail that fails to reach the addressee will be returned: many householders, receiving what is clearly a direct mail envelope addressed to the previous occupier, will throw it away; even if some do forward it the first time, they will not go on doing so indefinitely if the addressee, having received the first forwarded piece, does not then notify the list owner of his or her removal.

v) Where a "gone away" *is* notified, the database owner may find it worth while to send a special letter (in a plain envelope, marked Please Forward, and *without* a return address) to the old address, enquiring of the addressee's whereabouts; this may be forwarded and elicit a response.

What, then, about databases where the persons listed are not receiving goods through the mail, are not subscribers to a club or service, and are not being regularly mailed? A partial example, at least, of such a situation would be one of the life-style databases described in the previous chapter: the entries are up to date at the time the questionnaire responses arrive, and deteriorate thereafter. It is of course true that the names from these databases are mailed, as a result of list rental activity, and no doubt the database owners will make appropriate arrangements with the mailers for the return of gone away information. But such databases are mailed piecemeal – some elements very frequently, others hardly at all. One possible answer to this dilemma is to have one's database checked periodically (ideally annually) against the electoral register. Most companies that offer to rent selections from the electoral register are capable of offering this service too, and this does at least tell one, each Spring, who *was* living where as at the previous October. What it does not do is to indicate where any previous occupier may have moved to; as a result there is no way for the database to know that the Mr J Smith on whom it possesses ample information, but who no longer lives at 3 Acacia Avenue, Bedford, is the same person as as the Mr J Smith now revealed by the electoral register as having recently taken up residence at 16 Laburnum Grove, Aberdeen. In consequence, a database whose only means of maintaining addresses is an annual electoral register check, is continually losing data about persons who move. Even if the individuals concerned are subsequently picked up again, their past history will have been lost.

As with "gone aways", having once learned from the electoral register that an individual has moved, one can write to him or her at the old address with a request for forwarding; no doubt this will produce some results. The only other hope on the horizon is that the Post Office, which has been considering this issue for some time, may eventually be prepared to play a part by producing lists that link individuals moving house from old address to new.

**b) Business**   As in a number of other areas, the problems of name and address maintenance are somewhat different, and in some respects more difficult, when one is dealing with businesses rather than consumers. That consumers change address every eight years on average, creates problems; these are as nothing compared with the difficulties posed for business databases where any or all of the following can occur:

A business changes its address.
A named executive moves company and is replaced.
A named executive changes his or her job within his or her company, and is replaced in his or her former job.
A named executive changes his or her job title, and/or his or her reporting structure, but not his or her function.

A company change of address is probably less frequent than a consumer change, and no more problematical. But keeping check on who within a company is doing what job (and, even worse, what are the decision-making functions, in practice, of different jobs/ individuals) can be a nightmare. For this reason, much business-to-business direct mail is addressed to a job title rather than a person. There is available in the market-place a much wider variety of well-defined business lists than there is of consumer lists: if you are a manufacturer of widgets, it is not unreasonable to suppose that you can identify, and reach with fair precision, every company in the country that is a potential user of widgets – whether such companies be defined by standard industrial classification, by area, by turnover, by number of employees, by capital employed, by profitability, or by some combination of these. In some cases list brokers will offer to rent such business lists complete with named chief executives, or whatever. But if you want to mail named financial directors, or sales managers, that is likely to call for (expensive) research – probably by telephone. And keeping the information up to date once you have it is difficult – unless you have a sales force that is in regular touch with the companies concerned, or unless your personalized communications through the mail are such as to give addressees an incentive to inform you of changes – for example, if you are supplying periodicals. Otherwise, it may be back to the old device of the annual questionnaire.

## 2  Privacy

We dealt with one aspect of the privacy issue in the previous chapter, where it was pointed out that to hold data about an individual person on a computer without registering with the Data Protection Registrar was a criminal offence; this makes it mandatory to complete registration formalities before starting to collect data. Even after this has been done, and even where the database is operated in a manner consistent with the Data Protection Act, there are still on-going issues not covered by the Act, which, broadly speaking, relate to individual privacy. Thus, the Advertising Association's Code of Practice, referred to above, on data protection, states (Part III para. 5.2):

> "Even though the Act does not state that data subjects have a right to have their names excluded from mailing lists, the Council of Europe's Recommendation on Data Protection and Direct Marketing proposes that such a facility should be made available. Accordingly, data users to which this Code applies must comply with the requirements of the Code of Practice of the Mailing Preference Service and should, where possible, use the recommended method of not erasing the name, but of retaining it on file with a suppression marker."

What this means is that all database owners who are using their databases for consumer mailings have an obligation to subscribe to the Mailing Preference Service (MPS)*, and to mark appropriately on their databases the names of any persons who have indicated to MPS that they do not wish to receive direct mail promotions. Subscription to the MPS is not a legal requirement (MPS is a creation of the industry itself) but it is sound common sense. Much irritation has been expressed in the newspapers by people who receive what they regard as unreasonable quantities of direct mail advertising. A lot of this irritation is factitious (newspapers have their own strictly commercial reasons for disliking direct mail) but the cry that unsolicited mail constitutes an invasion of privacy, however pompous, silly, and over-the-top it may sound, can result in further legislative interference in commercial life – unless those involved in advertising by mail can demonstrate a serious and effective commitment to sensitive handling of public complaints. MPS is an attempt to demonstrate such commitment, and as such it should be supported, if only because the likely alternative will be very much worse.

## 3  Personalization

In the early days of direct mail, virtually all mailing pieces were directed to their destination by a name and address label, either stuck to the outside of the envelope or applied to some part of the mailing in such a position as to show through a window in the envelope; the letter inside would then start "Dear Sir/Madam" or perhaps "Dear Customer" or "Dear Reader". With the advent of clever computers, and even cleverer programmers, it became possible to contemplate producing letters which started "Dear Mr Jones"; testing showed that such "personalized" addressing produced significantly better response. Today it is a virtually universal characteristic of computerized mailing systems that they offer the facility to personalize letters – not only by adding a correct salutation, but by varying any part or parts of the text of the letter as may be required, by reference to the individual data found within the subject record. The advent of laser printers has greatly assisted this process, in consequence of their immense speed (compared to the old line printers) and enormous flexibility (e.g. ability to vary type fonts and sizes, and to print sideways, or upside-down).

Take for example, the case of an insurance company wishing to offer a life policy to a number of existing policy-holders who have house and contents policies only. A few years ago, prospects of this

* The address of the MPS is is 26 Eccleston Street, London SW1.

kind would have received a fairly bland letter, with a personal salutation to be sure, but otherwise undifferentiated between one person and another. And a leaflet would be enclosed with separate male/female age tables which the punter would have to examine to see what his monthly premium would be. Today age tables are all but redundant; indeed each letter can be tailored to the individual's circumstances, and can say, for example:

> "In return for this security, your monthly premium, at age aa is only £x per £1,000 of cover – so that you can, if you act NOW buy £100,000 of life cover for only £y per month. (Of course, if you were to delay that decision for just another b months, the premium would rise to £z per month.)"

As with everything else, there is a price to be paid for personalization. If you spell a person's name wrongly on an impersonal address label, he may be irritated, but this is unlikely to affect his judgement of your message. If your letter addresses him as "Dear Mr Fairy" rather than "Dear Mr Fairlie", your chances of business are probably less, from this individual, than if you had addressed him as "Dear Customer". And if you have referred to his age as 27, when he is in fact 54, then your pitch is hopeless.

There is, of course, no way of securing complete accuracy of data. But there are rules to be observed which will minimize risk:

a) No data should ever be permitted into a database unchecked. In the early days of computers it was regarded as axiomatic that all data was double-keyed: one clerk punched data into a punched card, and a second verified what was punched by re-keying. In these days of direct entry from keyboard to computer, this process is all to often ignored. Sometimes the system itself can check: as we have seen already, addresses can be checked, and even corrected, by reference to the Postal Address File. Names for given addresses can be checked against the electoral register (if the system has access to it). And so on – but a check of some kind there must be.

b) Systems themselves must be tested and checked. It is quite easy to program a system that will take

A. Jones Esq.,
3 Acacia Avenue,
Malden,
Surrey.

and produce a salutation "Dear Mr Jones". But what does the system do when presented with:

Admiral Sir Rodney ffotherington-Jones Bart., KCB

You might be happy if it printed either "Dear Admiral" or "Dear Sir Rodney", or even "Dear Sir" But less so if it came up with "Dear Mr KCB" or "Dear Mr Bart" or even "Dear Mr Admiral". Analogies to all of which I have seen in my time. In practice, of course, no system can be expected to cope optimally with all possible variants: the good system is one that will handle correctly 99.9% of cases, but will recognize the other 0.1% where it is out of its depth, and thereupon will fall back on "Dear Customer", or some other catch-all. This principle runs all through the personalization business: programs *have* to have a fall-back position for use in any case where the required bit of personal data isn't there, or can't be analysed by the rules available. It is in the ignoring of this principle that some of the funnier foul-ups – invariably reproduced in the press – occur.

c) Apart from names and addresses, most data in a marketing database is fixed – in the sense that if it is correct at the time of input, subsequent events are not going to alter it. There are, of course exceptions, which can usually be handled quite simply if thought about in time.

d) But although data about past events is fixed, information about present events is not – and both demographic and psychographic data fall into this category to varying degrees. Demographic data derived from the electoral register – such as size and composition of household – will date unless checked at intervals against the new register (which is itself published some five months after its data is collected). Data derived from the census can only be checked every ten years, and is only published two years after its original collection. But by far the most difficult problem relates to life-style information supplied in response to questionnaires by consumers themselves: clearly, the longer the time-lapse since this information was supplied, the less reliable it is. The ideal answer might be to repeat the same questionnaire to the same consumers annually: one company holding a rather specialized database does just this. Ibis maintains a database of academic staff at universities world-wide; annually it writes to each person listed in each university calendar with a questionnaire about their academic subject areas, and receives a very high rate of response. The case is no doubt unusual, because the individual concerned stands to benefit: the promise made by Ibis is that, when academic publishers mail book promotions through the Ibis database, those persons with recorded interests appropriate to each book will be selected, and those without, will not. In the absence of a similar incentive, it is not clear what sort of response to a regular questionnaire could be achieved – of course direct incentives of a more commercial kind are not ruled out, as with the original collection of data. Repeat questionnaires also have the obvious advantage of verifying addresses, at least for responders. But the total cost of the exercise is fairly high – say 20 pence per person addressed, or 25 pence per response, given an 80% response rate. How important it is to update demographic and life-style data – or how much cost it is worth incurring in the process – will in each case depend upon the uses to which the data is being put, and to the extent of personalization in the user's dealings with individuals on the database.

## 4  Postage

A word should be said on this subject for the benefit of those who will be addressing mailings to prospects on their database, because the need to maximize cost-effectiveness in this area may dictate decisions regarding database design. To post a thousand promotion pieces by second-class mail at the basic 60-gram rate, costs £150. This is a very large proportion of the total cost of perhaps £350 which each thousand mailing to a consumer list might be expected to incur. (Nevertheless, it is the relative stability of postal prices in the 1980s which has been the largest single factor in the increasing cost-effectiveness of direct mail – in contrast to its main media competitors, whose costs have grown much faster – and in consequence for the rapid growth in direct mail activity.)

Moreover, for many years past the Post Office has been prepared to offer a substantial discount, or rebate, from public tariff to bulk mailers (which basically means those with single postings in excess of 4,000 items) who meet certain terms and conditions. Various schemes of this kind were introduced over the years in a rather piecemeal fashion; in 1987 the Post Office announced its intention to rationalize these schemes under the generic title of Mailsort. A broad description of this service follows.

**a) Mailsort**  The Mailsort service comes in three different varieties: Mailsort 1, Mailsort 2, and Mailsort 3. Choosing which service to use depends upon optimizing three linked factors:

Speed of delivery
Cost of postage
Pre-posting sortation

Mailsort 1 offers the same level of service as the first-class letter-post, with a discount from first-class prices that improves as volume rises; in return the user must meet certain sortation and presentational requirements which reduce the workload of the Post Office. Mailsort 2 operates on the same principle, save that the service offered is that of the second-class letter-post, and the discount is from second-class prices. Mailsort 3 also works from the baseline of second-class letter-post prices, but the service offered here is delivery within seven working days. The percentage discounts available vary for each of the three services, and within each service will vary again according to the level of sortation achieved. In the case of all three services, some level of sortation must be undertaken before handing the mail over to the Post Office; basically, the lower the net price that you wish to pay for a given level of service, the more stringent are the sortation requirements. All sortation for Mailsort is based on postcodes.

Perhaps the most interesting departure from previous Post Office practice is the introduction under Mailsort of a sliding scale of charges for increasing weight of items over 60 grams, rather than the traditional "stepped" scale, as currently used in the public tariff. The effect of this new departure, illustrated in the diagram below, is to give a substantial saving – even before applying the Mailsort discount – to mailers of letter-post items weighing anything over 60 grams. As can be seen, the saving widens as the item-weight increases.

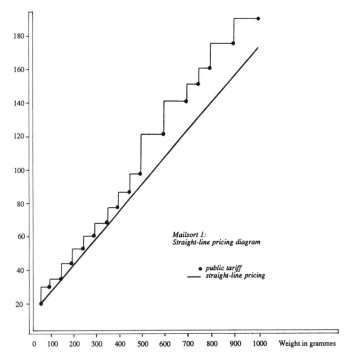

*Mailsort 1:*
*Straight-line pricing diagram*

● *public tariff*
—— *straight-line pricing*

Weight in grammes

Mailsort 2 & 3:
Straight-line pricing diagram

● public tariff
—— straight-line pricing

To take an example, a piece weighing 61 grams would cost, under second-class public tariff, 24 pence; under Mailsort 2 or 3 it would cost 15.1 pence, less whatever discount was allowable for sortation undertaken. At 601 grams the difference is between 110 pence at public tariff, and 88.6 pence before discount under Mailsort. The overall effect is that, under Mailsort 2 or 3 one is paying an extra 0.136 pence for each gram over 60. A ready reckoner for this straight-line pricing system is available from the Post Office.

The formula for calculating the correct Mailsort price (pre-discount) is as follows for Mailsort 1: [(Weight of item in grams – 60) x 0.175] + 20p. And for Mailsort 2 and 3: [(Weight of item in grams – 60) x 0.136] + 15p.

The discount available from the straight-line Mailsort tariff varies according to the level of sortation achieved, with a top rate of 32%. To earn these discounts, the mailer must meet a number of conditions, of which the most important are:

i) Mail must be sorted according to a sortation plan based on postcode.

ii) At least 75% of all items must be correctly postcoded, with at least the outward code. (This percentage will be increased to 85% *fully* postcoded at January 1990, and 90% ditto in January 1991.)

I have not attempted to deal here with all the details of Mailsort:

this is not a how-to-do-it book, and further details can be had from your postal sales representative*.

The important point for present purposes is that anyone seeking to collect information in a database and to use it for mailing purposes must take account, in the data collection, and in the database construction, of the requirements of the postal system – and therefore of the need for postcoding and for mail sortation.

**b) Postcoding**   Since postcoding is going to be an essential feature of any database which is to be a source of bulk mailings – quite apart from its other marketing advantages that we have examined in Chapter 4, Section 1 b above – it is relevant to consider here the alternative possible approaches to postcoding for a database owner. There are two aspects of postcoding to be considered: how to add postcodes to an existing large collection of names and addresses, and how to ensure that new addresses, as they are added to the database day by day, carry correct postcodes with them.

By far the simplest answer to the first problem is to use a bureau. A number of computer bureaux now have programming systems capable of taking bulk addresses in a very wide variety of formats, analysing them, looking them up on the Postal Address File (PAF), correcting some types of error, and allocating the correct postcode. Unanalysable or ambiguous addresses are, of course, rejected for clerical scrutiny.

Nor is it necessary – at least for consumer address files – to conduct an exhaustive survey of which bureau has the best system, or offers the best value for money. The Post Office, which has an obvious interest in maximizing the use of postcodes, has given its seal of approval to postcoding systems run by a number of computer bureaux.* Better still, the Post Office will actually meet the computer bureau costs of any firm using one of these Post Office-approved systems to postcode a file in excess of 20,000 addresses. (The Post Office will *not* meet the cost of any residual necessary manual postcoding.)

What remains to be determined is how to handle the residue of rejected addresses that the computer system cannot deal with. In the case of consumer addresses, any of the Post Office-approved systems should be readily able to postcode accurately upwards of

---

* Additionally, copies of the Mailsort User's Guide, edited by the present author, are available from the Post Office on request to Royal Mail Marketing Department, 33 Grosvenor Place, SW1, Tel 01 235 8000.

* A list of these firms is available from the Royal Mail Marketing Department.

80% of addresses submitted to it. (The actual percentage achieved is much more likely to be a reflection of the condition of the original data than of the competence of the particular system.) In the case of business addresses, whose format is more variable and more complex, it may well prove beyond the capacity of many postcoding systems of a general nature to postcode more than 60%, and those with complex business databases may well find that it pays to look for a bureau that specializes in, and has a record of, dealing with such cases, since systems developed primarily for consumer addresses are likely to perform rather poorly on business files.

Even in the consumer case, this still leaves a substantial proportion of addresses that the computer system can't handle; there remain three possible courses of action:

Put them on file un-postcoded;
Throw them away;
Take clerical action to postcode, and re-insert.

The first alternative is feasible only so long as the proportion of un-postcoded addresses then appearing in bulk mailings from the database does not infringe Mailsort requirements (which will also become more stringent over time: see subsection a above). Nonetheless, it seems to me an undesirable option, leading as it does to an untidy and ill-disciplined database which fails to take full advantage of all its potential assets.

Manual postcoding is expensive. Each address has to be looked up in the Post Office's Blue Books (the printed equivalent of the PAF) and the very fact that the computer has failed to recognize them means that a high proportion of them will be pretty troublesome. Some will probably be untraceable by anyone less skilled than the local postman – and sometimes by him too. The cost of this exercise must be borne by the database owner, since the Post Office will only meet computer costs of postcoding. Nevertheless, the sensible course with computer-rejected addresses will usually be a mixture of the second and third options: manual look-up of all, with a judicious discard of those that are time-consuming beyond a certain point.

Adoption of such a policy means that one's choice of bureau, from among those certified by the Post Office, should be governed by consideration of the quality and price of its services in relation to manual postcoding of the expected computer residues. Clearly it is desirable to use a bureau that will itself perform the total exercise involving both computer and manual phases, presenting its client at the end with a clean and comprehensive result.

Solution of the second problem – how to cope with ensuring the accurate postcoding of day-by-day additions to the database – is liable to be more problematical. If the database owner intends to have his database built and maintained by a bureau, then matters are reasonably simple: one chooses a bureau that is possessed of appropriate postcoding software, and specifies that, in addition to the one-off postcoding of the existing collection of addresses, the system must contain the facility to postcode each incoming new address prior to adding it to the database.

But if database owners propose to run their own database in-house on their own computers, then they must do one of two things. Either they must build their own "front-end" postcoding system to analyse and postcode new incoming addresses; this will include purchasing a copy of the PAF (and an updating service for the same) from the Post Office. Alternatively they must seek to find a bureau which can supply a software postcoding package that they can incorporate into their own system. The former course is a very substantial systems undertaking, which involves re-inventing not just the wheel, but the internal combustion engine as well. The latter is preferable, but the range of choice is not wide.

For those who are possessed of a small database, to which there is not a large quantity of daily new input, there is another possibility. The PAF is now available on CD-ROM (standing for Compact Disk, Read Only Memory).* A PAF in this format can be loaded on a CD-ROM reader attached to a microcomputer (if the database concerned is on a micro) and used by the operator as a sort of sophisticated microfiche reader, to call specific addresses to the screen, from which the associated postcodes can be read off, and entered on the keyboard.

---

* Available from Silver Platter Information Ltd, who produce the PAF/ROM, and also from Computer Factors Ltd. who market it, particularly in conjunction with their database system Mailbrain.

# 6 Data Selection: Regression

## 1 Consumer Lists

In the days, still not so far distant, when data of any kind about individual consumers was scanty, and hard to come by, the business of despatching a direct mail promotion involved searching out such lists of names and addresses as could be found to which were attached some characteristic which could be held relevant to the matter in hand. This business of marrying lists of names, via some one characteristic to marketing campaigns, is still the staple of the list-broking trade. So, one can rent a list of members of the British Film Institute, a list of commodity investors, of purchasers of thermal underwear, or buyers of specialized chrysanthemums. Nothing save this one characteristic is known of the people making up those lists – other than their names and addresses.

Most of the time making decisions to mail to anyone other than one's own past customers used to be a matter of hit or miss – or at least of trial and error: if you were in fact successful in selling microcomputers to buyers of thermal underwear, it was much more likely to be because the list was well-maintained, up to date, not over-exploited, and composed of persons already accustomed to buying through the mail, than because of any product affinity.

A direct mail company with its own list of past customers was in a similar if somewhat better position: customers who had bought one thing from the company were probably quite good prospects for another thing – and better still if the "things" bore some relationship to each other. As the amount of data on customer lists (one can scarcely call them databases at this stage) started to grow, so companies started to distinguish between past customers – on the basis of time elapsed since last purchase, or type of goods bought, or speed of payment, or some such. The distinctions were "broad-brush" and based on common sense, or at any rate on observation. It might come as a surprise, for example, (at least to a non-gardener like myself) to discover that buyers of a truly encyclopaedic gardening book, far from being poor prospects for yet another gardening book, were actually superb prospects. Gardening enthusiasts, it appears, actually *collect* gardening books, as insatiably as lepidopterists collect butterflies. And the same is true, only more so, of cookery books. But, surprising or not, the phenomenon was readily observable, and, being observed, easy to adjust to.

As the amount of data available on customer lists grew, so the problem of classifying groups or individuals according to their probable propensity to respond to this or that offer became more complex, and through the 1960s and 1970s organizations like Consumers' Association, the Automobile Association, and Reader's Digest, with huge mailing programmes and ever-increasing banks of information were forced into developing fully-functioning databases. Even then although the software available for selecting names and addresses on the basis of extremely complex algorithms was sophisticated, the actual methods for determining what the algorithms should be, hadn't advanced at all: it was still a matter of common sense, or guesswork, or trial and error.

The first breakthrough came in the early 1970s, with the availability of census data from the 1971 census on magnetic tape. For many years past Reader's Digest had been using the electoral register (in printed form) as a source of names to whom it could offer magazine subscriptions. In fact the electoral register was the only source of names large enough to supply Reader's Digest's immense mailing campaigns (which had to sustain a magazine circulation at that time of one and a quarter million UK subscribers). With this background, Reader's Digest was the first company to undertake the expense of converting the electoral register itself to magnetic tape. But how to determine whether any given addresses or groups of addresses from the register were better or worse prospects than any others, was still largely a mystery.

The census data, it was felt, might provide the key. But how to use this amorphous mass of information? Some of it was probably relevant, and some possibly so – for example the information that such and such an area had a 30% higher proportion of children than the national average, or a large concentration of houses with two bathrooms. But relevant in what ways? Was *The Reader's Digest* dominantly read by persons with children, or by persons with two bathrooms, or both? And what about the information on persons travelling to work by motorbike – was that, too, significant? And if one's instinct was to say No – how could one be sure? Harder still, might it not be the case that *combinations* of particular data items would be found much more significant than each item singly might lead one to suppose?

The answer was to be found in a collection of mathematical

techniques that the industry, incorrectly but conveniently, has come to lump together under the general heading of regression analysis. Since this book is not a mathematical treatise, and hopefully will be read with profit by many who might flinch at a mathematical symbol, we will follow common industry practice and refer hereafter to regression analysis *tout court*, without being particular as to whether we are dealing with what the mathematician would recognize as a multiple regression process, or discriminant analysis, or principal components analysis.

The problem can be stated in this way: we have a group of people – potentially the whole adult population – about whom we have a wealth of statistical information. We want to use this information (if we can) in order to predict, for each of these people, their relative propensity to behave in a particular way – in this case to respond to a particular mailing.

And the methodology can be described in some such way as this. First, we take a representative random sample of our universe – and it *does* have to be representative, or the whole exercise is invalidated. Then, we expose this sample to the same mailing as that we are enquiring about. (The size of the mailing should be such as to bring in not less than 500 responses.*) Mark the record of each respondent. Then submit this "model", consisting of all the sample records, together with the statistical information available on each, to a regression program. This will analyse the characteristics (in this example our statistical census data) associated with each respondent in the model in order to deduce what combination of characteristics best distinguishes between respondents and non-respondents.

The result of this process will be to produce a formula which can be expressed along these lines:

$$\text{"Propensity to respond} = a.x + y\,b - \frac{z}{c}\text{ " (or some such)}$$

where x, y, and z represent characteristics of the record (in this case census variables), and a, b, and c are constants assigned by the regression program.

The next step is to put the whole universe which the model represents through a further program which will evaluate each individual record against the computer formula, in order to determine each person's relative propensity to respond. This propensity – or "score"

* For a much fuller discussion on the mathematics of random sampling, see Chapter 4, *The Royal Mail Direct Mail Handbook,* published by Exley (2nd ed. 1989) by the present author.

as we may now call it – is simply expressed as a number: the higher the number, the greater the propensity. Finally, the computer will produce a statement of the score distribution of our universe, showing what percentage of the total has a score of x, x+1, x+2, etc., together with a statement of the average percentage response to be expected from the highest-scoring 10% of the list, the next 10%, and so on. This enables one to select and mail only those parts of the list that are predicted to respond at or above a given level.

So much for the theory. In practice some short-cuts are required. No one, for example, would attempt to use all 4,500 census variables in a regression analysis of this kind: even to record such a mass of information against all 24 million households in the country would result in an absurdly large file, and clearly many of the variables are redundant (through irrelevancy, or duplication of effect) for marketing purposes. Moreover, a full regression analysis employing this number of variables would occupy an inordinate amount of computer time. Even where each extra variable adds something to the accuracy of the result, the law of diminishing returns is inexorable, and after a while "improvements" become minimal, and not worth the increasingly high cost.

We have already seen* that the major bureaux handling demographic data use between 38 and 104 census variables for the purpose of grouping census enumeration districts into homogeneous "clusters", and a similar "boiling down" of census data – again using mathematical techniques – is a prerequisite of any use of such data for regression purposes.

In effect, of course, the demographic type (as described by Acorn or one of its competitors) into which a given household falls already represents a generalized distillation of the census variables; many advertisers are content to determine (by analysis of a sample mailing) that response to their effort comes predominantly from certain Acorn types, and thus to ensure that further mailings are directed to those types. Or, of course, the Acorn type itself can become one variable, along with purchase behaviour and life-style data, to a regression process as described above.

Some advertisers are frustrated by the lengthy process of performing a sample mailing, waiting for, and analysing, the results. From this has grown the practice of analysing the demographic characteristics of existing customers on one's database, and selecting as new prospects those with similar characteristics. This is a highly dangerous practice, amounting to a form of in-breeding. If, by way of example, your present database contains a very high proportion of people

---

* See Chapter 4 Section 2.

living in Acorn Neighbourhood 15 (Council Estates, Well-Off Older Workers), is this really because this is the type of audience that is attracted by your offer, or is it because your earlier advertising has been particularly concentrated – perhaps by mere accident – on this type of person, possibly through selective use of press media, or through geographic concentration, or whatever?

A real-life example may serve to make the point. A magazine publisher, selling subscriptions to his general-interest title, was very concerned to discover that his subscribers were heavily weighted to the over-35s. Did this mean that his editorial material didn't have sufficient appeal to younger people? Was he not in serious danger of losing circulation as his existing subscribers grew older and died off? Or would those now younger than 35 take to his product in greater numbers as they in turn reached the magic age? And if so, why – what was the trigger? The answer was laughably simple: the publisher was recruiting new subscribers by mailing offers to heads of households from the electoral register; not surprisingly young adults were grossly under-represented in his advertising campaign, and hence among his subscribers. The age profile of the subscribers on his database had nothing – or at least nothing ascertainable – to do with the nature of his editorial material, or the appeal of his offer, but everything to do with the built-in bias in his previous advertising universe.

Regression analysis in a marketing context began, then as a way of discriminating better from worse prospects on a very large list (the electoral register) by reference to very large volumes of data (census variables, or at least a selection of them). The techniques are, however, generalized, and can be used on any list of any size where the individual records have any number of variable characteristics. Basically the regression process is simply a way of constructing, from a quantity of variables, an algorithm for selecting those individuals most likely to behave in a certain way. The process is fairly cumbersome, and, if done properly, may require a lot of elapsed time. But the improvement that it makes to response, compared with "common-sense" methods of constructing algorithms, will increase rapidly with the number of variables to be considered. If there are only half a dozen variables, each with a small range of values, for each individual record on the database, then it isn't difficult, by intuition or experience – or after a cursory glance at the results of a sample mailing – to construct a near-optimum formula for selecting the worthwhile prospects. But where we run into dozens, or scores, of variables, each with a potentially wide range of values, regression (otherwise referred to, with less offence to mathematical niceties, as modelling and scoring – a term which is not committed to any particular collection of mathematical techniques) becomes an essential tool.

Finally, then we can complete our picture of a marketing database. As indicated in the earlier database diagram on p.41, a database as I have defined it consists of data, computer hardware, and computer software. The data may include some or all of:

Information derived from sales or enquiries
    (including names and addresses);
Demographic data
Life-style data

The software must allow for address handling (including post-coding and postal sortation), for profiling and reporting on the information contents of the database, and for selection of records from it. This selection in turn should be capable of being activated either by an algorithm based upon record contents, or via a modelling and scoring exercise. And the whole might be diagrammatically represented thus:

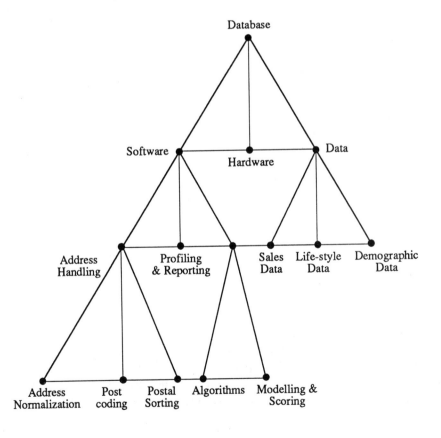

## 2 Business Lists

The problems of selection for mailings to businesses whose records are held on a business database are substantially different in practice – even though much the same theoretical considerations apply – from those of consumer databases. Looking again at the diagram above, of the five main triangles appearing there, two will require modification if the diagram is to describe a business-to-business marketing database. Starting first with the Data triangle, clearly life-style and demographic data are not relevant to the description of a company. The sort of data we might hold in a business database could be represented thus:

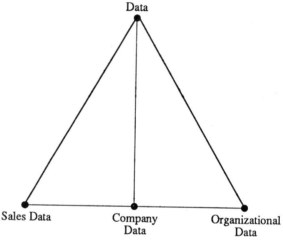

The sales data, as in a consumer database, would deal with the advertiser's two-way relationship with the prospect. Company data would typically include such items as:

Standard Industrial Classification (SIC)
No. of Employees
Size of Premises
Type of Premises (e.g. Head Office, Branch, Factory)
Turnover
Advertising Expenditure etc.

Organizational data might include names and job titles of individual executives, perhaps with functional descriptions and an indication of reporting structure.

Secondly, the Selection triangle in a business database representation would effectively disappear. Selection criteria for business-to-business mailings are normally fairly simple, and, with rare exceptions, will not call for such advanced techniques as regression analysis: a fairly simple algorithm will do the job perfectly well. The prime problem with business direct mail is not one of knowing to which prospects a given approach should be made, but rather one of understanding, within each prospect company, the decision-making processes – a task rendered much harder by the fact that these same processes can change overnight with a change of personnel – without, necessarily, any visible change in structure taking place. In the case of a consumer database, data collection and data maintenance, while rarely simple, can usually be reduced to a routine; in business databases they are an art form. By contrast, selection processes for consumer mailings demand constantly renewed ingenuity, and inventiveness at a high technical level; in the case of business mailings, such is rarely the case.

# 7 Planning a Database

## 1 Introduction

Let me try to summarize to this point. The increasing affluence of today's consumer society has created a market-place that is rapidly fragmenting in such a way as to render older mass-marketing techniques increasingly expensive. The effort in consumer marketing to distinguish one's *real* prospects from the undifferentiated mass is increasingly important. In the first instance this has resulted in a realization that those persons who have already differentiated themselves by becoming customers have, in so doing, provided a wealth of valuable information, which must be retained – and maintained. These past customers are not only the best possible prospects in themselves; analysis of their behaviour can provide invaluable insights into the direction to be taken by one's marketing to new prospects.

Nor are those whose marketing efforts are directed towards other businesses exempt from these trends. As businesses increasingly specialize – or form specialist divisions – to cater for the fragmenting market, so their own needs and interests reflect the specialization of the consumer market they are trying to serve; the marketing effort of their suppliers needs to take account of this.

The extent to which businesses in the past have ignored information laid before them by their customers – utilizing only what was required for the delivery of goods, or the creation of an accounts receivable, and discarding it when these necessary functions were performed – is truly astonishing. But that time is now passing. In order to be able to collect, retain, maintain, and use information about past customers, companies require access to database techniques. And in order to be able to pinpoint new markets with the greatest possible degree of precision, the same is true. And direct mail in turn is either the major means, or at the least a valuable secondary means, through which an investment in database can be rendered profitable – and indeed through which the database can be maintained. How then should a marketing director plan his company's approach to database marketing and direct mail?

## 2 Strategic Planning

The first step in building a database – as in any other long-term business project – is to produce a strategic plan, that begins with a consideration of objectives – in this case the overall marketing objectives of the business, followed by a definition of the audience to be reached in pursuit of those objectives. The next step is to ask what purpose(s) in relation to those objectives the putative database is intended to serve; the plan will then go on to consider:

Data Availability and Sources
Hardware and Software Needs
Database Structure
Data Capture
Data Verification and Enhancement
Database Design
Data Maintenance
Data Analysis/Selection/Reporting

Similarly, a direct mail campaign must derive from the company's overall marketing objectives and the nature of the audience it is addressing. Consideration of these factors will make possible a statement of direct mail objectives, both overall and for a particular campaign, followed by:

Definition of the Market
Creation of Promotion Material
Production of Promotion Material
Creation of a Selection Algorithm
Selection of Names
Addressing
Enclosing and Despatch
Response Handling

These strategic overviews can be represented diagramatically, in a way that also shows the connections between the two types of activity, as indicated in the following diagram:

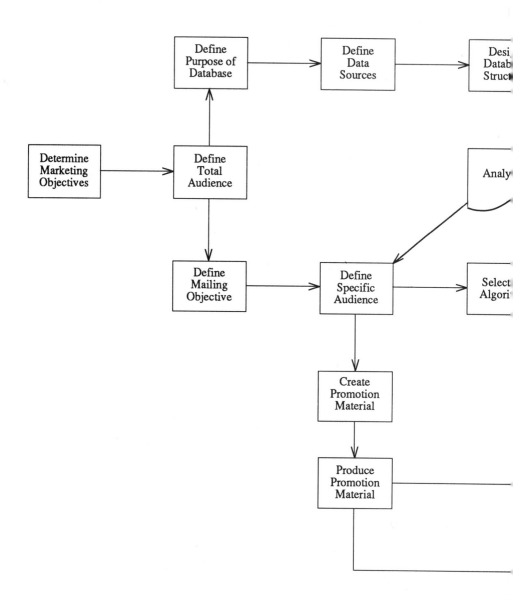

This diagram shows a central database which initially is fed with accumulated data from sources both inside and outside the company. Maintenance of the data is ensured by two separate feedback systems – the provision of database information and analyses to a sales-force, which responds with details of its customer-related activities; and

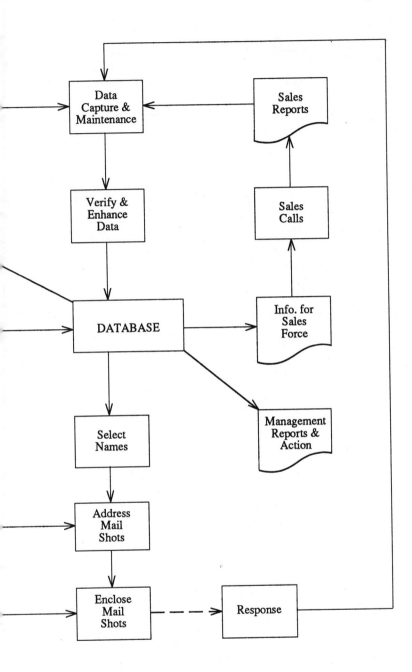

the handling of response to direct mail material addressed to persons on the database. Clearly, not all database applications will possess all the functions here shown; the important point is that some kind of maintenance mechanism, performed here by these two feedback loops, is essential.

## 3  Hardware

Having defined a database at an earlier stage in this book as comprising hardware, software, and data, we have reached this point where a good deal has been said about the data, a little about the software required to handle it (and there is more to come on this subject in a moment) and virtually nothing about the hardware.

This isn't a book about computers, so we will not spend too long on the subject, or become technical. But it does seem desirable to address briefly the question, which arises time and again when considering the construction of a database: what kind of, or how much, computer capacity is needed to support a marketing database? In this form, of course, the question sounds like asking how long is a piece of string; nevertheless some guidelines can be given which may assist in providing answers for particular cases, even though there is no generalized formula to fit all needs.

The question most commonly asked in this area is how much hardware capacity is required to run a database, or perhaps, more specifically, can one run a database on a microcomputer. I will address the first question, in the hope that in answering it, so far as that is possible, light may be shed on the second question also.

First, then, let us examine the constraints that operate, under each of the following heads:

Storage
Processing Speed
Multi-user Facilities
Print Capacity
Communications

**a) Storage**  Any serious database application involving more than a few hundred records will require hard disk memory: there is no future in trying to run a database of any significant size on floppy disks. If we consider records consisting only of names and addresses, it should be possible to store up to 4,000 records per megabyte (one million bytes) of disk space. This figure should be reduced for business addresses, which are typically longer than consumer addresses, and in any event assumes that the software in use permits variable-length records, and variable-length fields within records: if this is not the case, there will be large quantities of wasted space caused by catering for maximum-sized records, and fields within records.

For a consumer marketing database with name and address plus other data, one would typically be down to 2,000 records per megabyte – but even this figure assumes no waste space; it is also desirable that the software used be able to pack and unpack data in binary form where this is logically feasible.

Current hard disk storage on micros can be taken up to 175 megabytes – which is probably a greater capacity than one would wish to use for a micro-based database, on account of other constraints. If the maximum sensible size for a database on a micro is felt to be not much more than 200,000 records, this would require disk capacity of 100 megabytes – or more if the records are particularly long. On mini, or mainframe, computers, where the other constraints (which we discuss below) are less pressing, and where the amount of memory available seems almost unlimited, the size of database that can be handled is scarcely a problem, so far as mere memory capacity is concerned. Even on a micro, given the amount of storage now available, plus the probable further extension of this in the near future, it is much more likely to be other factors that impose limitations: a substantial further leap in the processing power of even today's micros will be required before their full potential memory capacity can be used.

**b) Processing speed**   There are two aspects to this: the speed with which an individual record can be called to the computer's screen, and the speed with which sequential records can be processed – e.g. in the course of a selection run.

i) It is desirable that any required record reach the screen in a time not exceeding two seconds. (That may sound very fast, but in fact for an operator sitting at a keyboard, delays that sound quite trivial can be devastating in their effect on productivity.) Current-technology micros can achieve this on databases under 200,000 records – although the extent of multi-user processing (see below) is a potentially limiting factor very hard to assess.

ii) Great strides have been made recently in micro processing speeds; with the latest technology equipment it should be possible to handle in excess of 100,000 records per hour – five or six times as many as could have been achieved just a few years ago. This does, however, assume the use of software capable of fairly sophisticated data structure – in particular the separation of static data such as name and address from key selective data, together with appropriate cross-indexing. This still means that to select from a database of 200,000 records will take two hours on a micro. I would regard that as a sensible limit.

**c) Multi-user facilities**   2-5 user systems (that is, systems where 2-5 operators, each with a screen and keyboard, can use the same computer at once) are not uncommon nowadays even on micros. It isn't really possible to set a theoretical limit – one leading software house claims to be able to provide a 40-user micro system – should anyone want one. Clearly a lot depends on the level of activity by each user, and, if activity is other than constant, the extent of "bunching"; the greater the activity at any one time, the greater the probable consequence in slowed response time. Any user contemplating going to, or extending, multi-user facilities *must* begin by simulating worst-case conditions on an actual installation.

An alternative approach is to link two or more micros in a local area network, in which they share access to a single database. This might make sense where individual users required substantial processing capacity, but relatively infrequent access to the database. However, the single-machine approach is to be preferred wherever it is feasible.

**d) Printing capacity**   The advent of desk-top sheet-fed laser printers has been a boon to micro users. These machines are quoted as being able to print up to 500 sheets per hour. However, they are essentially small office equipment, and not an adequate solution to volume printing – e.g. of names and addresses from a database. The only sensible answer here is still a line printer, or continuous stationery ink-jet or laser equipment; these cannot be driven by a micro as of now; this means that large-scale output has to be transferred in magnetic medium to a bureau with a mainframe or mini driving a suitable printer.

**e) Communications**   Transferring data requires a suitable medium of transfer. Of course, data transfer by floppy disk is feasible; it will require access to a facility for transferring data from floppy to some mainframe medium such as nine-channel magnetic tape. More interesting is the recent advent of a conventional magnetic tape unit that can be linked direct to a micro: this makes bulk communication between micro and mini, or mainframe, a simple matter for the first time.

The concepts discussed above can in principle be handled on any IBM-compatible micro equipped with hard disk storage: the most basic level, in terms of cost being an Amstrad 1512 at something over £1,000. Clearly there will be additional costs for printing facilities, communications, multi-user stations, etc as required.

## 4   Software

It is convenient to distinguish under this head two different kinds of software: that which is completely generalized and application-independent, and that which is needed to perform the particular application of an individual user.

Under the first head we may distinguish first the computer's own operating system, which need not detain us here: on a micro, most of which are IBM-compatible, it will be a variation on IBM's DOS (Disk Operating System). There will also, for anyone wishing to run a database system, be some form of DBMS (Database Management System), comprising both the program that allows one to structure a database in the computer's memory, and the language through which users can access the database.

A number of database users have started with a proprietary DBMS, incorporating an operating system, and then built their own particular application software to go with it. The alternative approaches to this course are:

a) to purchase from a software house a software package that, with a greater or lesser amount of customization, and a greater or lesser degree of compromise over user requirements, can be adapted to do the job;

b) to go to a computer bureau with a specification for the building of a database system. The bureau will then have the same options of building a wholly particular system from scratch, or of adapting an existing package. The user will also have the choice of having the bureau run the system on its own hardware for a shorter or longer period, and of bringing it in-house onto his/her own hardware earlier, later, or not at all;

c) as a subset of either of the above solutions, some software houses, and some computer bureaux, offer a "turnkey" service: that is to say, they offer to provide to their clients a total working system incorporating the hardware and the software to meet their needs, installed on their premises, and up and running, complete with training facilities for their staff.

Which of these options it is best to adopt, will vary from case to case. The larger and more complex the database application, the less likely it is that users can find a suitable package that will, even after customization, meet their needs. If, in addition, users already have a substantial computer installation, and a systems and programming staff, then they may feel that the best course is to develop their own system in-house. This will depend, however, on the degree of priority which they can command within their in-house systems teams: systems departments tend to have a long queue of jobs and over-stretched resources. Where this is the case, the bureau option may be quicker and involve fewer problems all round. The question of whether the system, once developed at a bureau, should run on the bureau's hardware or not will be a simple matter of weighing up in-house computer capacity and bureau cost. We will discuss in a later chapter the criteria that need to be considered in choosing a particular bureau.

For smaller and less complex databases it should be possible to find appropriate packages which, with some customization, will fit the bill. There is not, at time of writing, a wide range of choice on the market, but there are a few good offerings. At the bottom end of the size/complexity scale, the question of where to run the database scarcely arises, since even if the necessary hardware has to be purchased from scratch, the costs are relatively trivial. (Printing is another matter: if bulk printing is required, and facilities are not available in-house, then use of a nearby bureau for this limited function is likely to be the best answer.) Therefore, where we are talking about a database system to run on a micro, for example, then however the software is obtained – by in-house development, by purchase, or by development at bureau – the supposition must be that it will ultimately be run in-house on the user's own micro.

## 5   Economics

The diagram in Section 2 above indicates the planning steps that are a necessary prerequisite to the creation of a marketing database, and to the despatch of a direct mail shot addressed to selected promotees from such a database. What it does not deal with is the cost-benefit question: how does a company determine in the first place that building a database will be beneficial – which means that it will improve the profits of the company.

Too many cost-benefit studies that are done to justify investment in business and industry are over-ambitious, and their conclusions thoroughly bogus. Much of the work done in this area is derived from American models, and is infected with the transatlantic assumption that no concept is worthwhile until a precise numerical value has been put to it – and conversely that any concept to which such a value has been put, has thereby acquired a sanctity of precision in which the dubious and wholly imprecise methodology by which that value was guesstimated in the first place can be conveniently forgotten.

The approach of those who favour this model is to identify every foreseeable consequence, negative or positive (cost or benefit) of the course of action being examined, and to follow it through to its second or third order outcome, tagging each manifestation with a precise value. These values are then summated, and a series of impressive-looking calculations is produced to show the expected discounted cash-flow effect of any particular decision over a period of time, the return on capital employed, and the effect on a series of annual P&L figures.

The difficulty with this approach is that not all costs and benefits are equally forecastable; consequently, while some of the figures in the calculation will be accurate, others may be wide of the mark by several hundred per cent, and still others – even without allowing for incompetence on the part of the compiler – may be overlooked altogether.

In the case of most investment decisions – and certainly when we are considering database investment – the costs are more readily quantifiable, in fairly precise terms, than the benefits. This fact provides the clue to my own preferred method of conducting cost-benefit analyses – a method which keeps the relative uncertainty of this or that piece of data constantly before the reader, and indeed the writer, of the analysis.

This method, then, begins by laying down the criteria against which the course of action being examined is to be judged – for example that the negative cash flow from the project must at no time exceed £x; that there must be a cumulative positive cash flow by month y; that there must be a return on capital employed, from month y onwards, of not less than z% per annum. There may be other alternative, or additional, criteria, some or all of which may not be of a directly financial nature – relating perhaps to staff employment, or to standards of customer service, or whatever. They should all, where they are critical to implementation of the course of action in question, be clearly spelled out at the outset; this is, of course, a policy-making function.

The analyst, having been given these criteria, should then begin by estimating the *costs* of the course in question. In the context of database, these will include the costs of:

Hardware
Software – purchased, or developed in-house
Staff Training
Data Capture
Data Enhancement – by postcoding, Acorn coding, etc.
Data Maintenance
System Usage – time & materials of operators & users

The analyst should then ask, in the light of these costs, what are the *minimum* financial benefits that the system must earn in order to meet the pre-ordained criteria, and determine what likelihood there is of the system being able to produce those benefits, on the required scale. This will provide a first-order idea of whether the scheme in question is viable or not. If it does appear viable, then the analyst should go back over the figures, adjusting anticipated costs upwards to the *highest* levels that seem probable, and ensuring that the claimed benefits really are the *lowest* that are likely to be achieved. If, on the other hand, the initial analysis seems unfavourable to the project, then the opposite course should be followed: the analyst should then consider whether the conclusions would remain the same if costs could be shaved (without straying outside the bounds of probability) and if savings above the minimum level could be achieved.

The purpose of this proceeding is to ensure, if possible, that the recommendations one makes will remain valid in the circumstances least favourable to them. At all events, if the recommendation is that the project studied should proceed, then the quantified benefits should be kept as close as common sense permits to the level required by the criteria laid down. If thereafter the analyst wishes to gild the lily, it is possible of course to say:

> "On the basis of these minimum level benefits – and assuming maximum probable costs – this project will meet its targets, and should therefore proceed. It should however be observed that certain benefits have been estimated on a deliberately conservative basis; it is reasonable to hope that a further benefit of x might, on a more optimistic view, result. Furthermore, certain other benefits will certainly occur, whose precise financial implications are wholly unquantifiable, but still real. These are..."

Of course, the difficult situation is the one where a project cannot satisfy its predetermined criteria on a fairly pessimistic set of assumptions, but can do so, perhaps with a margin, on a modestly optimistic set. Let us illustrate the point by a somewhat simplistic example:

The project is to set up a database for the Customer Care Department (better known as the complaints department) of an organization which has to deal, by letter and telephone, with members of the public. By giving each clerk in the department immediate access via a keyboard and screen to a computerized database, it will be possible to provide a much quicker and more customer-friendly service. The criteria that have been laid down for judging the viability of this project are:

a) Capital invested must not exceed £100,000.

b) Net negative cash flow (excluding capital items) must not exceed £50,000 cumulatively at any point.

c) There must be a cumulative positive cash flow (excluding capital items) from the project within one year from its commencement.

d) During Year 2 and subsequently, net savings from the project must be sufficient to provide interest on the capital employed at the rate of 20% per annum or above.

Let us suppose that our costs look like this:

Capital cost of hardware and software: £50,000 in month 1.

Other one-off costs chargeable to P&L: £10,000 per month from month 1 to month 4 inclusive.

Running costs: £10,000 per month from month 3 onwards.

This will give rise to a negative cash flow picture like this:

| | MONTH | | | | | | | | | | | |
|---|---|---|---|---|---|---|---|---|---|---|---|---|
| | 1 | 2 | 3 | 4 | 5 | 6 | 7 | 8 | 9 | 10 | 11 | 12 |
| One-off Costs £ | 10K | 10K | 10K | 10K | | | | | | | | |
| Running Costs £ | | | 10K | 10K | 10K | 10K | 10K | 10K | 10K | 10K | 10K | 10K |
| Cum. Costs £ | 10K | 20K | 40K | 60K | 70K | 80K | 90K | 100K | 110K | 120K | 130K | 140K |

Let us now suppose that we are confident of being able to generate minimum quantifiable savings (through improved labour productivity, reduction in repeat complaints as a result of faster handling, etc.) amounting to £10,000 in month 5, £12,000 in month 6, and £15,000 per month thereafter. Adding this to our cash flow, gives a picture like this:

| | MONTH | | | | | | | | | | | |
|---|---|---|---|---|---|---|---|---|---|---|---|---|
| | 1 | 2 | 3 | 4 | 5 | 6 | 7 | 8 | 9 | 10 | 11 | 12 |
| Cum. Costs £ | 10K | 20K | 40K | 60K | 70K | 80K | 90K | 100K | 110K | 120K | 130K | 140K |
| Savings £ | – | – | – | – | 10K | 12K | 15K | 15K | 15K | 15K | 15K | 15K |
| Cum. Savings £ | – | – | – | – | 10K | 22K | 37K | 52K | 67K | 82K | 97K | 112K |
| Cum. Net £ | (10K) | (20K) | (40K) | (60K) | (60K) | (58K) | (53K) | (48K) | (43K) | (38K) | (33K) | (28K) |

On this basis, we are failing to meet two of our criteria: there is a negative cumulative cash flow in excess of £50,000 for two months, and the arrears have still not been cleared off at the end of year 1. (On the other hand, return on capital employed, once the arrears are paid off, is at 60% per annum.)

Now assume that this is the rock-bottom position, and that we have reasonable confidence that, with some effort, the savings position could be improved to something like this, transforming in the process the negative aspects of the earlier picture:

| | MONTH | | | | | | | | | | | |
|---|---|---|---|---|---|---|---|---|---|---|---|---|
| | 1 | 2 | 3 | 4 | 5 | 6 | 7 | 8 | 9 | 10 | 11 | 12 |
| Cum. Costs £ | 10K | 20K | 40K | 60K | 70K | 80K | 90K | 100K | 110K | 120K | 130K | 140K |
| Savings £ | – | – | – | 10K | 12K | 15K | 18K | 18K | 18K | 18K | 18K | 18K |
| Cum. Savings £ | – | – | – | 10K | 22K | 37K | 55K | 73K | 91K | 109K | 127K | 145K |
| Cum. Net £ | (10K) | (20K) | (40K) | (50K) | (48K) | (43K) | (35K) | (27K) | (19K) | (11K) | (3K) | 5K |

Further, the analyst may reasonably add that no credit has been taken for the effect on the company's reputation, and hence on its sales (and particularly repeat sales) of better customer service. Only a fool would attempt to put precise figures to such benefits – but equally only an idiot would deny their reality. What is now required is a management decision on how to balance the stringency of the original criteria against the degree of confidence in achieving the better savings target, together with the expectation of added unquantifiable benefits.

This method does not eliminate the uncertainties involved in investment decisions and project management. Far from it: by highlighting the areas of uncertainty, and trying to put high/low estimates on them, rather than attempting to clothe every guess in a make-believe garment of mathematical exactitude, it puts the difficult decisions back where they belong – in the hands of those responsible for policy, rather than in those of the technicians, who too frequently have an axe to grind.

**Summary**  What, then, are the areas in which one should look to achieve benefits from a database – not just in the type of example quoted above, but more generally?

a) In the context of direct mail selling, the prime benefit from a database must be the ability to secure business at a lower cost per order. Suppose the case where a company is mailing 100,000 prospects at a cost of £400 per thousand, and obtaining a response rate of 2% – i.e. 2,000 orders, at a cost of £20 per order. It might be that database techniques would enable the user to distinguish better from worse prospects on this list, and to mail, say, 50,000 prospects only, getting a response rate of 3%, or 1,500 orders, at a reduced cost per order of £13.33. Alternatively, if the total available list were larger than 100,000, it might be possible still to mail the same number, but different groupings, giving a response rate of, say, 2.5%, equalling 2,500 orders at a cost of £16 per order.

b) In the context of the type of business-to-business activity where a team of salesmen is employed, the objective of database techniques is to improve the salesmen's productivity by improving the scheduling of calls, thus obtaining more calls per salesman's week, and, by providing information, and by the use of direct mail back-up, to improve the effectiveness of calls. These objectives, added together, amount to more business at lower unit costs.

c) In the context of telesales – either where the telephone is being used by the seller to contact his prospects, or where ordering by telephone is a facility being offered to prospects at their discretion – a database to which the telesales team has immediate access provides a wonderfully simple basis for taking orders, checking credit, accepting credit card payments, etc., with the least possible delay and fuss. Indeed one might reasonably say that such a database is today an indispensable prerequisite of a successful telesales operation.

d) In the context of a retail operation, a database, supported by direct mail advertising, aims to increase the level of traffic in the operator's shop(s), again with the object of increasing total business while reducing the average cost per sale. Further than this, analysis of the database will enable the operator to draw conclusions, with greater precision, about the nature of his clientele, which may stand him in good stead when it comes to opening new outlets, choosing advertising media, and so on.

e) In every context, a database of customer records lightens enormously the burden of handling customer queries and complaints – both those that arrive through the mail, and, even more significantly, those that come by telephone. Indeed, an on-line database makes it, for the first time, easier, quicker, and cheaper, to deal with queries over the phone than by letter – an enormous benefit (even if one hard to quantify in cash terms) for buyer *and* seller.

# 8 Finding Help

Advertisers who have followed the argument thus far, may have concluded that they ought to set about determining what database marketing has to offer them in their particular circumstances, and how they might embark on the task of creating and using a database. They will now wish to know how they can most economically, and with the best hope of reaching the right answers, get started on such a course.

It is a major theme of this book that neither database marketing, nor direct mail which is one of its more significant weapons, is a thing-in-itself: database marketing, and direct mail, are properly employed only as part of an integrated marketing strategy. This means that the review of database potential, and plans for its implementation, must be approved at that level of management, and by those persons, responsible for designing such overall strategy. This will normally mean the marketing director, and appropriate members of staff, together with their advertising agency. This in turn raises the question of whether advertising agencies in general are competent to advise on – or to assist with – database projects, and/or direct marketing. To this question there is, sadly, no simple answer.

## 1 Advertising Agencies

Over the last few years, most of the major advertising agencies have found it expedient to build, or acquire by purchase, a direct marketing arm, department, or subsidiary. In some cases this represents a genuine, if late, recognition that direct marketing (and direct mail in particular) is the fastest-growing advertising medium there is, and still a long way from saturation point; in other cases it is more of a defensive reaction, to pre-empt the possible loss of restive clients who want to come to terms with these new developments.

In addition, there are agencies that specialize in direct marketing, either in the sense of undertaking nothing else, or in the sense of running an integrated all-media activity which nonetheless obtains a very large share of its total turnover from direct marketing.

Quoting names in the agency world is always a risky business, owing to the mercurial way in which agencies form, split, and reform with bewildering, kaleidoscopic rapidity. But Ogilvy & Mather is a good example of a large main-line advertising agency that has in recent years become a very significant force, world-wide, in direct marketing, having, in the UK, acquired by purchase a specialist direct marketing arm now known as O&M Direct – previously Trenear-Harvey, Bird, and Watson. Contrariwise, The Yellowhammer Advertising Company is an outfit presenting a single face to the world while making a very large part of its living in direct marketing. Amherst Direct Marketing, as its name implies, is about direct marketing *tout court*. (I will not tempt the libel lawyers by pointing the finger at specific outfits whose direct marketing activity consists of one man and a boy contracting out client work to other, more competent, shops. They do exist, and, once warned, advertisers should have little difficulty in spotting them.)

For many advertisers the rational choice of agencies will lie between going to a specialist direct marketing agency, on the grounds that that is likely to offer the greatest direct marketing skills, and going to (or sticking with) a non-specialist with genuine skills in a variety of fields, on the grounds that this will offer the best marriage of different media. Just to complicate matters, there is another dimension to the choice.

A traditional advertising agency's role is to devise an advertising strategy for its client, to perform the creative function of translating that strategy into words and images for a single- or multi-media campaign, and to book media space. The production of print-media advertisements, or the shooting of film, will be contracted out. With direct mail, most agencies have reckoned to follow a similar path, doing the strategic thinking and the creative work, but sub-contracting the printing, addressing, enclosing and despatch. The difficulty with this approach is that in direct mail, to a degree not experienced with other media, the development of new production methods for handling the "mechanical" functions of printing etc. turns these functions too into reservoirs of creative ideas, that are relevant to copy-writers and designers – and indeed to strategic planners. This means that a purely "creative" agency, that isn't regularly exposed to production concepts, has rather little chance of being in the forefront of new ideas in direct mail. Naturally the good agencies are aware of the potential problem, and take care to see that their creative staff do have proper exposure to, and training in, the use of the latest production facilities. But the interface between what can often appear like two cultures isn't always a smooth one – the more so when the two are embodied in different organizations. This is one reason why some advertisers will go not just for a specialist direct marketing agency, but for a "full-service" agency – one, that is to say, which will perform in-house all of the following functions as required:

Consultancy
Creative work
List Broking
Computer bureau work (incl. Database management)
Four-colour printing
Laser printing
Enclosing and despatch

Even then, of course, contracting out may be required: a shop that offers four-colour printing will not necessarily have all the relevant facilities of a specialist printer, for example. But at least within the four walls of a full-service agency there can be found all the types of skill required for a successful direct mail campaign.

The choice then can be expressed as whether to go to a specialized or a generalized agency, and if the former, whether to opt for the creative house that seems to have the best possible approach to one's problems, or to choose from the small number of full-service houses that have a wider range of skills at their direct disposal – but may not necessarily be the ideal choice over every sector in question.

Of course, there is no single ideal answer. Some agencies have carved out niches for themselves in particular areas – such as financial marketing – where they may have acquired a lead in understanding of sectoral problems which would make them an almost mandatory choice for particular clients, overriding other considerations. Or, it may be that the advertiser's need to exploit sophisticated formats, and equipment for handling such, is paramount, so that he or she feels the need to be with a full-service agency where complete understanding of all the factors involved may be found between one set of walls. Certainly, if he or she intends to get involved in database construction it will be essential to be with an agency that employs computer-literate staff who, if not themselves involved in database construction, can at least look after the client's interests adequately in this specialized field.

Where a company already has substantial advertising expenditure in conventional media, my own preference would be for appointing a single agency to handle the advertising across all media – taking care to choose an agency that has established and verifiable direct marketing skills of its own (including, where database is involved, computer expertise). I would also be anxious to know to what extent direct marketing was properly integrated into the agency's work, in terms of strategic planning and detailed creative thinking: this is still an unsatisfactory aspect of very many agency operations, where the need to have a direct mail operation has been recognized, but the need to integrate its activities has not.

## 2 Consultancy

Where, for one reason or another, integration of direct marketing or database activity with other media advertising is not an issue, a specialist direct marketing agency is likely to be the better choice. Whether this should be a full-service agency (where the real choice is rather small) or not, will depend on individual circumstances. In any event, the advertiser may wish to consider using initially the services of a consultant to help map out an overall database and direct marketing strategy, and to assist in the choice, and perhaps the subsequent control, of one or more service houses to carry out the work. While an advertiser who is using a major agency will not require to employ a consultant as well (since consultancy is precisely part of what an advertising agency is about), an independent consultant may well be of value in guiding an advertiser through the maze of specialist houses and full-service agencies whose various activities we are about to examine in more detail. The particular activities which a direct marketing consultant should be able to perform in conjunction with the client are:

perform a cost-benefit study of the construction and use of a marketing database;

produce a document in the form of an invitation to tender for one or more computer bureaux;

choose bureaux to be approached;

evaluate bureaux tenders and make recommendations regarding the creation of a database and the subsequent activity on it;

monitor the work of the successful bureau to completion;

advise the client on how best to implement the agreed uses of his new database; in particular to advise, with regard to direct mail activity, on the strategy to be employed, in terms of the products to be offered, the audiences available for them, the pricing structure likely to prove effective, and the overall results achievable;

advise on those houses best qualified to assist in the creation of direct mail campaigns and material for this particular advertiser;

monitor the work of the selected service houses.

Of course, not all of these functions will be required in all cases: for example, some advertisers, having determined to create a marketing database, may well wish to design and build this in-house, using their existing data processing team and computer resources. We will be examining the pros and cons of this approach, so far as it is possible to do so in general terms, in Section 10 below. That apart, it will be seen from the above list that the consultant's function – as distinct from that of the traditional advertising agency – is to perform a series of one-off tasks, rather than to enter into a continuing long-term relationship with the advertiser; the object is to enable the advertiser to become self-supporting in a new form of enterprise, as quickly as possible.

An advertiser, then, who wishes to get into database marketing and/or direct mail, who has decided not to use a main-line advertising agency as a primary mentor, but who requires services from one or more of the specialist houses available, may consider using a free-lance consultant, one of whose major tasks will be to guide the client through the choice of helpmeets from the areas we will now proceed to consider.

## 3 Creativity

The word "creative" and its various derivatives is one of the most abused terms in advertising. Every type of operator in direct marketing needs to be creative, in the sense of finding new ways to use the tools of the trade to solve new problems, or to provide more profitable answers to old problems. Yet the "creative department" in a full-service direct marketing agency will always be taken to mean those employed in copy-writing and design, as though they alone were possessed of this curious faculty of spinning original ideas out of the ether.

In direct marketing, as in any other form of marketing, the most important variable by far is the product on offer, and after that, the audience to whom it is offered. A host of other criteria will, or may, affect the outcome of a sales campaign – the price, incentives, such as a free premium, or a prize draw, credit facilities, and, of course, the words and pictures in which the whole package is expressed. Changing, or even just modifying, the words and pictures can significantly enhance the profits of a campaign, or even change a potential loss into a profit. And since it is usually easier to change the words and pictures than to change a product, or a target audience, and less risky than to change a price, it is frequently on the words and pictures that attention is lavished, sometimes to the detriment of more fundamental issues.

The same high profile is given to the so-called creative functions in terms of the industry's own educational initiatives. It is, I suppose, scarcely surprising that books and articles on direct marketing tend to be written, in disproportionate numbers, by copy-writers, who are also among the more articulate, and entertaining, performers on the lecture circuit. But attention to words and pictures can be overdone – indeed is so habitually overdone in our industry that it is necessary to introduce any discussion of this important function by pointing out that they are neither all-important, nor even the most important feature of the direct marketing (or any other marketing) scene.

The reason for this over-estimation of one small sector of the industry, is that it is a sector which every more-or-less literate person believes they can understand and criticize, preferably without having to think too hard – something certainly not true of list development, or database structuring, or computerized fulfilment. This attitude can lead to a heresy the very opposite of over-estimation – that of supposing that since we can all handle the English language, basically anyone can write their own sales copy.

About this let there be no doubt: no copy-writer or commercial artist will make a long-term success out of a dud product, or a good product offered to the wrong audience, or at the wrong price. Equally, the right product at the right price, facing the right audience still needs a professional copy-writer and designer to do it anything like justice, and it would be a dire mistake to attempt to avoid this process.

So, where does one go for copy-writing and design services? First, it must be emphasized that copy-writing for direct mail is not at all the same thing as copy-writing for, say, a press ad. No doubt it requires the same basic talents, but the experience that goes to making a skilled direct mail copy-writer can only be acquired through work in that specific field. Advertisers who use an advertising agency with a direct marketing department/subsidiary should have to look no further; advertisers who are in search of a direct marketing agency will look in the first instance for one with a high creative reputation.

One of the first tasks in choosing a service house (creative or other) is to discover which trade associations it belongs to, and whether or not it is 'recognized' by the Direct Mail Services Standards Board (DMSSB) – the independent body concerned with standards in direct mail advertising, and particularly in service houses. An advertiser considering using a service house that is not recognized by the DMSSB, should take steps to find out why not – there may be quite acceptable reasons, but they should be sought. Of the trade associations, the one that takes the most trouble over vetting applicants for membership is the Direct Mail Producers Association (DMPA). Historically this has been an Association for lettershops and fulfilment houses (see below) but an increasing number of creative houses are now in membership. Some houses specialize in working for particular types of client (for example, one creative house may have substantial experience in financial services marketing); the DMSSB or the DMPA may be able to help with advice in this area – although the latter's first loyalty is, naturally, to its own members.

Once one has a short list of suitable creative houses, choosing between them should be no different in principle from choosing any other supplier. Ideally, houses on the short list should be invited to study a brief prepared by the advertiser or his consultant, and to respond with a presentation. Some creative houses will only consent to give a presentation if they are paid for the work involved. This is, to my mind, deplorable – however, a house that can afford to take this attitude is clearly not one that is worried by a dearth of clients.

In addition to securing a presentation, the advertiser should visit the service house's premises. (This rule should apply to *every* service house employed, or considered for employment, on the campaign.) The advertiser should make it clear in advance that the presentation is to be conducted by the people who would actually work on the account: too many accounts are won by a touch of brilliance applied by some senior person who is never seen again after the presentation. Arising from presentation and visit, the advertiser should ask himself these questions:

a) Has the creative team properly understood the brief?

b) Are the creative ideas in the presentation adequate, sound, novel, or exciting?

c) Are the team assigned to the account compatible with the operation?

d) What other clients does the creative house have that have relevance to this assignment? (One or two references should be taken up. Since it is most unlikely that the house will name as referees anyone likely to give poor references, what one has to look for is the *degree* of enthusiasm or satisfaction expressed.)

e) Does the house have other accounts that might pose problems for it in working on this assignment – e.g. close competitors?

Some of the longer-established, or larger, houses will have their walls lined with certificates of award-winning feats. These are the agencies whose creative people turn out copy and art that is considered pleasing by other creative people. No doubt some of it makes money for the advertiser, but awards are no guarantee of this. There are not too many direct mail awards won by Reader's Digest creative team: they are too busy counting the money.

It is normal (though not invariable) for the creative house, whether or not it is a full-service agency, to undertake responsibility on the client's behalf for the post-creative operations required to get a campaign into the mail. These post-creative functions we will now consider one by one, before going on to look at the functions, not specific merely to one campaign, that are required for the construction of a database.

## 4   The List Business

The list business is by far the most fraught, and the least satisfactory, part of direct mail activity. For those who propose simply to create a database from their own customer records, there is no problem, since they need have no dealings with list brokers – unless and until they may wish to use list-broking services to market their database for others' use. But those who wish to acquire prospect names, with or without discriminating information, or those who wish to enhance the information on their own customer files, by reference to demographic data, or other information in the public domain, will find themselves drawn into the world of list broking. In this world there are a number of players:

a) **List owners**   These are the people who have proprietary rights in one or more lists of names and addresses, nowadays almost invariably held on some computer-readable medium. These may be, for example, lists of subscribers to a particular publication (from which can perhaps be inferred a particular occupation, or specific interest) or of persons who have bought this or that (range of) product(s) through the mail, or members of a particular society, or persons whose names appear on a public register of some kind (electoral register, register of shareholders, etc.) Business lists exist, both of companies engaged in this or that trade or business, and of persons practising this or that profession; these belong to whichever party has taken the trouble to compile them from published sources.

**b) List brokers**   Although there are companies that compile, and themselves market, their own lists, (the compilers of life-style lists, as discussed in Chapter 4 Section 3 above being an outstanding recent example), most available lists in fact belong to owners for whom the revenue derived from list rental is strictly a side-line or by-product. These owners find it convenient to market the use of their lists through a list broker (sometimes on an exclusive basis, sometimes not) who will advertise the availability of the list, and act as a go-between for the parties involved in its rental, in return for a commission, usually expressed as a percentage of the rental charge, paid by the list owner. Direct mail advertisers who wish to acquire the use of a list will resort to a list broker, who will produce a catalogue of available lists, with a brief description of the charac- teristics of each, an indication of price, and a statement on the restrictions governing its use (e.g. most list owners prohibit rental of their lists to their competitors).

**c) List managers**   In many cases there is an intermediate party be- tween the list owner and the list broker – namely the list manager. By this term I mean to designate (because it is not always used in the same sense) the party that actually controls the physical list, and is responsible for its maintenance, updating, etc. Frequently, of course, this will be the list owner himself; sometimes it will be the list broker; in some cases list owner, manager, and broker will be one and the same entity. But it is not unusual to find that the list owner has delegated list management functions to a computer bureau, and list broking activities to a separate list broker, creating a chain of three parties with whom the direct mail advertiser will have to do business. Indeed the three may become four: if the list broker whom the advertiser first approaches finds that the ideal list for his client is broked on an exclusive basis by another broker, then both brokers will be in on the act (and share the commission).

This division of responsibilities, together with the system whereby all intermediate parties are obtaining their fees from the list owner rather than from the advertiser, gives rise to all sorts of difficulties, running the whole gamut from dishonest practice to simple incom- petence. (There are, of course, honest *and* efficient operators in the list business, but this is an area where the old adage of *caveat emptor* applies, in spades.) I will try to indicate some of the more problem- atical issues.

Lists, in the direct mail business, are rarely, if ever, bought and sold: they are rented, usually for one-time use. Different list owners impose different conditions on the circumstances surrounding such use. The most common condition is that the list cannot leave the premises of the list manager in computer-readable format: it must be reproduced onto a printed medium before the advertiser, or the lettershop working on his behalf, lays hands on it. The thinking here is that, whereas an unscrupulous person might be tempted to copy a magnetic tape, the cost of data-capturing printed names and addresses is likely to be an effective deterrent (and too many people would have to know about it). For a few list owners this is still not enough, and they will insist that the list, in whatever medium, shall not pass through the hands of any party they have not approved. The list owner's final protection (for there are dubious operators on the other side of the fence as well) is to "salt" the list with names and addresses of employees, using, perhaps, bogus initials, or some such device whereby mail addressed from that particular list can be recognized, and any unauthorized use of the list spotted.

Such caution is understandable. What advertisers must not permit is that these proper precautions prevent them from assessing for themselves the quality of the list they are renting. It is a curious feature of the direct mail industry that lots of hard-headed businessmen, who would not dream of paying substantial sums of money for products that they couldn't inspect and check, will nevertheless take on trust – at least until disaster strikes – a wide range of services without any serious attempt to verify that they have been performed effectively, or even at all. When renting a list, there are, first, a number of questions that must be asked, and which the list broker *should* be able to answer. They are:

i) How was the list compiled? (i.e. from what source, and by what methodology). In most cases list compilation at some stage involves data capture by a person at a keyboard. It is important to be clear whether one can rely on a reasonable standard of accuracy. Moreover, lists composed of persons known to have responded through the mail are superior to lists sharing similar characteristics in other respects.

ii) How often is the list mailed by the owner, and for what purposes? If the owner is mailing frequently, and/or with expensive material, then there is a clear incentive to ensure list cleanliness.

iii) How often is the list mailed by others? Very frequent use, particularly by the advertiser's competitors, may erode responsiveness. On the other hand, it may indicate a trustworthy product – can references be obtained?

iv) What sort of feedback exists to the list from persons addressed from it? If it is a list of (paid) subscribers to a journal, for example, addressees have an incentive to call for correction of errors. At the very least "gone aways" returned by the Post Office should be regularly processed against the list. (In this context, frequent list usage may be an advantage.)

v) What allowance is the list owner prepared to offer in respect of "gone aways" incurred by the advertiser? For some time it has been standard practice to offer to refund the postage on any "gone aways" in excess of a certain proportion (e.g. 5%). In my opinion this isn't good enough: the advertiser loses much more than the postage, whereas the list owner obtains (or should obtain) a positive benefit from "gone aways", which are a vital feedback to the list. It is interesting that at least one list owner (NDL) is now offering to pay a sum of money (which is greater than the lost postage) for each and every "gone away" returned. I hope that much more pressure will in future be applied by advertisers to ensure proper treatment in this respect.

vi) What proportion of the list is postcoded, fully and partly (i.e. outward code only)? Has the list been subjected to an automatic postcoding process? Postcoding simply copied from in-coming sources of addresses is liable to a high level of error, and is not, on the whole, a good indication of accurate addressing. On the other hand, the application of *full* postcodes by computer implies a very high level, among those items, of correct and viable addresses.

vii) Over what time-span has the list been compiled? What proportion of the total is more than one, more than two, etc., years old? Where we are dealing with a list that implies two-way traffic – e.g. a list of paid journal subscribers, or club members – this question is less important; in all other cases it has a large bearing on the probability of finding particular persons at the address given.

viii) What proportion of the list can be personalized – that is, addressed by correct title and surname? Not every advertiser will require this facility, but most direct mail letters today do attempt to provide a personalized salutation.

ix) It can be assumed that any consumer list consists of named individuals at private addresses. But in the case of business lists, the list may consist of company names and addresses only, or of job titles at company addresses (in which case it is desirable that the user knows whether these are the job titles that are known to exist within these specific companies, or are merely presumed titles – as if, for example, one were simply to assume that every company on one's list had a managing director, or a sales director). Or, again, one may have a business list where each entry has a named individual, complete with a specific job title. The need is to know, for any given list, what the true state of affairs is.

x) Can the list manager sort the list, prior to printing, into whatever sequence is required in order to minimize postal charges? (The implications of this question will become sharply greater with the introduction of the Post Office's new Mailsort system; indeed, there will then be a subsidiary question: what level of postal discount can the user expect, under Mailsort, once the list has been sorted by the list manager?)

Obtaining answers to questions of this kind is one thing; being sure that one can trust the answers given may be another. No advertiser should rent a list for the first time without having had sight of the actual names and addresses, or a sufficient sample of them, in printed form. This may have to be done on the premises of the list broker, or list manager – but done it must be. Of course, merely looking through a list of printed names and addresses will not tell one everything about the problems that may arise, but it will suggest a good deal. Here are some of the questions to which one should be alert in looking through a printed list of addresses:

i) How have titles/initials/first names been dealt with: are titles and either initials or first names always present; has any consistent presentation been followed?

ii) If the list is a business list, is the handling of individual names/ job titles as you have been led to believe?

iii) Are postcodes, full or partial, present in the sort of proportions you have been led to believe? Is there a significant number of clearly invalid postcodes?

iv) Are there invalid or incomplete addresses? (E.g. the omission of counties, where these ought to appear, would indicate that the list has not been through an automatic address-validation process, as would the appearance of a London address with no postal zone following it.)

v) Are there obvious mis-spellings, or other nonsenses? (Again, mis-spellings of post town or county names should indicate the absence of proper address-validation.)

vi) Having been satisfied so far as is possible from a visual inspection, the advertiser would be well advised wherever possible to test a small sample of any list being considered for rental with an actual mailing. This has a two-fold purpose: to further ensure that the list is what it seems, but also to determine whether it can produce the results hoped for. Such list testing isn't always possible: the list may be in total too small to make this a sensible option, for example – but it is an option to be weighed up and considered.

A good list broker will be able to advise an advertiser on the full range of lists available that may be relevant to the latter's needs – will be able, indeed, to propose creative ideas on the possible relationships between available lists, or segments of lists, and the needs of a particular campaign. This creative ability is perhaps the most important quality that the broker has to offer; the rest is simply the administrative skill necessary to any kind of broker, or go-between. And what must always be remembered is that the broker, although apparently working for the advertiser, is actually paid by the list owner: however honest the broker may be, and however anxious not to alienate the client, to whom it may be possible to make future sales as well, nevertheless the advertiser cannot rely on the broker to ask all the questions that should be asked, or to be determined to get meticulously accurate answers.

## 5  Printing

In the context of a particular direct mail campaign, the creative team may determine on their own the printing needs, and simply sub-contract the work to a competent print shop, who will have the function of producing the material, possibly finishing all or some of it (i.e. folding, collating, binding, stapling, etc.), delivering as required either to the lettershop that is to perform the enclosing function, or, in the case of the addressing medium (letter or whatever) to the computer bureau where the lists are held.

In some cases, however, knowledge of print equipment can be harnessed to the creative process to produce a new, or at any rate a non-standard, format. This is the kind of circumstance in which the creative agency with its own in-house print capacity will sometimes score, through being able to put together a multi-disciplinary team with minimum trouble. New formats apart, the print business is normally the least troublesome of all the processes to be considered in mounting a direct mail campaign. The problems that do arise tend to be not printing problems, but problems of co-ordination; too many printers (both individuals and companies) are still possessed of the craft mentality which allows them to take all manner of trouble over the application of their particular skill, while wholly ignoring the needs of other people, or even the dictates of common sense. Thus attention to numbers is frequently inadequate; boxing and transportation often careless, so that items arrive creased, or buckled; boxes come unlabelled; three items for a given mailing arrive on time, with the fourth delayed. And so on. Most reputable printers can be trusted to do a respectable production job; I don't know too many printers I would trust to do all the ancillary things sensibly and competently without strict supervision.

Where the creative house is acting as agent for the advertiser, and sub-contracting to printer and lettershop, this supervision should be its job. It is frequently (I had almost said usually) overlooked, leaving the wretched lettershop, which is at the end of the line, and has to compensate for everyone else's mistakes, to pick up the pieces. Or else the creative house waits until the lettershop screams, by which time it is usually too late to mount a fully effective rescue.

The moral is a simple one. Every direct mail campaign requires a detailed schedule of events – probably best expressed as a form of critical path diagram – showing what has to be done by whom and when. And even more urgently it requires a progress chaser (which means a person of character and some authority, not a junior secretary) to follow the process through, to prevent delays where possible, and to foresee their consequences where unavoidable. This job *can* be done by the advertiser, or by an agency or creative house. Too often it isn't, and a job, which may already have suffered delays at the creative stage, arrives at the printers where it splits into its component parts and overall control is lost. Those advertisers who decide to employ consultants do so in the knowledge that a substantial part of what the latter can contribute lies in their commitment to maintain control on ideas and material through the many stages, and many separate hands and heads, that they must traverse.

On the next page may be found an example (illustrative only) of a first-order critical path diagram. The scale along the bottom of the diagram indicates units of time; the right-hand edge of each box indicates, by its position on the scale, the earliest point in time by which the activity represented in the box can be completed; the "critical" path is represented by the *straight* arrows – that is to say, any slippage of any of the functions on that path will cause a slippage of the whole project; limited slippage on other paths will have no such effect. In real life, many of the boxes on this chart would

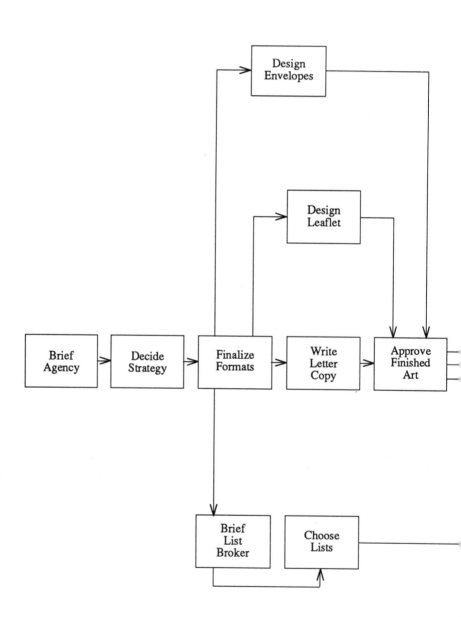

themselves have to be further analysed, and subdivided into component parts. For example, the process of writing letter copy will involve an iterative loop of writing, revising, re-writing, re-revising, gone through, it may be, many times; it will be necessary to check that the overall time-scale allows sufficient leeway for this.

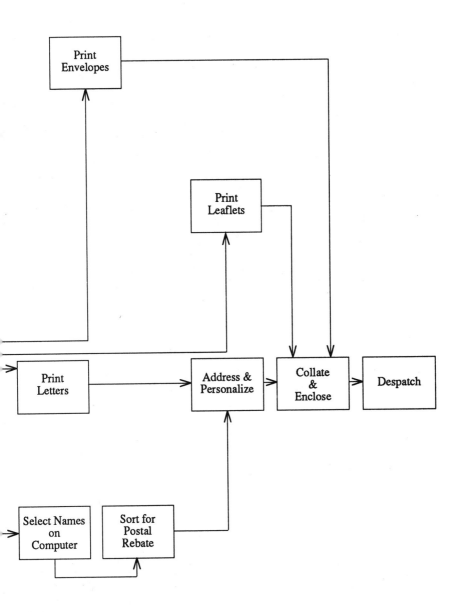

## 6  Sorting

The Post Office, for many years past, has offered discounts to bulk mailers who are prepared to observe certain terms and conditions, and to undertake some of the work that would otherwise fall to be done by the Post Office itself. The most important item in this context relates to sorting the mail for convenient onward transmission through the postal system. At the time of writing, the whole system of discounts and rebates – which has grown up over the years in a rather haphazard way – is being rationalized. The revised system, which goes under the generic title of Mailsort, has been outlined already above in Chapter 5, Section 4.

In order to earn Mailsort discounts, qualifying mail will have to be sorted according to criteria based upon postcode. We have seen already that this requirement imposes certain constraints on the construction of databases which are to be used for mailing, and on the handling of incoming data, so as to ensure that the postcode information necessary for sorting is present and accurate. What is important here is to recognize how the actual process of sortation has to fit into the overall business of getting an addressed mailing into the post.

Clearly the old-fashioned method of manual sortation into pigeon holes in sorting frames, as performed by the Post Office itself until recent times – and even now with certain types of mail – is inordinately time-consuming and expensive. It may still be the only available method for sorting mail addressed from non-computerized lists: such items will normally be sorted either after enclosing, or by sorting empty envelopes immediately before enclosing. We deal with these below in Section 8. But the largest, and still growing, proportion of lists are now held on computer, which renders relatively simple the task of sorting the name and address information in electronic form, prior to addressing. This task, then, has to be undertaken by the computer installation that holds the database, or list of addresses.

Mailsort will allow the postal user a considerable flexibility in the choice of sortation plan: the more comprehensive the sorting done, the greater the level of discount available – but the higher the costs that will be incurred, not so much in terms of computer processing, but in terms of the physical handling of the mailing subsequently, in particular at the lettershop, where the finer the sort, the greater the labour in bagging and labelling for despatch to the Post Office. Agreement on the level of sorting to be undertaken – and the level of discount to be expected – will have to be reached in the first instance between the advertiser (or an agent) and the lettershop; their agreement will then have to be conveyed to the computer processing house that will have to implement the required sortation.

The Post Office, wishing to make the transition to Mailsort as trouble-free as possible, has hired a computer bureau (CACI) to undertake the task of producing an embryo database which is available free of charge to any computer user wishing to adopt Mailsort sortation logic. This package, now in use at a number of computer installations, is universally available, and can be installed with little once-for-all effort for use on any mainframe computer installation. Thereafter, all mailings addressed from that computer installation can be produced in whatever version of the Mailsort requirements may be specified: current indications appear to be that little more computer time is required to meet Mailsort specifications than those of the earlier rebate system. The main change is the degree of consultation that will be required between the parties involved – particularly in the early days while the new system is still largely unfamiliar.

## 7 Addressing

Determining the mode of addressing for a direct mail shot is an important part of the original strategic design; it is closely bound up with the question of personalization, which we will also discuss here. Most direct mail shots are addressed to an individual person by name (or possibly by job title) either at home or at the place of work. The simplest way of achieving this in bulk is to print a series of identical letters, all with the salutation "Dear Sir or Madam", and to put the individual names and addresses on the outer envelopes. Few direct mail advertisers would consider this adequate today, for two reasons:

a) A direct mail shot should always carry a response medium. This may be a tear-off slip on the letter, or a separate business reply card, or anything else the designer cares to dream up. Ideally the response medium should itself carry the addressee's name and address as applied by the advertiser: it saves the punter from having to overcome inertia so far as to find a pen and fill in a form; it also ensures that the advertiser's reference data apposite to this particular customer will be present when the response comes back. This means that some response item *within* the envelope must be addressed.

b) Most direct mail letters today are personalized, at least to the extent of starting with a personal salutation: "Dear Mr Ramsbottom". To achieve this, the letters will have to pass through some form of computer printing which, even if it doesn't print the full letter text, will at least print the bits that differentiate one individual addressee from another.

The first of these problems was solved many years ago by the use of window envelopes: the response medium would carry the punter's name and address, which would show through the window – avoiding the problem of double-addressing envelopes and response media, not to mention the problem of correctly collating two separate individualized items.

The second problem, personalization, could only be solved on any large scale with the advent of computers. The computer could be programmed to print a personal salutation on the letter – what a waste then to be using a second operation to put addresses on a separate medium, re-introducing, incidentally, the collation problem referred to above. The most usual answer was to print the name and address at the top of each letter (this being standard practice for business letters in any case) followed by the personal salutation; to turn the top of the letter, bearing the name and address, into a tear-off response medium, and to let this show through the window of the envelope.

There still subsist, however, a variety of different modes of addressing, suitable for different circumstances. We will discuss here only those that involve at some stage computer printing from a magnetic tape, or disk.

**a) Cheshire label**   In this example the computer prints addresses onto plain continuous stationery. The addresses will appear with 1-4 items in parallel across the web, the number depending upon the particular type of machine to which the stationery must go after printing. This factor will also govern the depth of each label, from the top of one address to the top of the next – usually either 1″ or 1½″. This in turn will determine how many lines of address can be accomodated. After printing, the stationery, still in fanfold and with its sprocket holes, will go to a labelling machine. The first machines of this type were made by the Cheshire company in America, and first used in this country by Reader's Digest in 1964. Although Cheshire now has competitors, the name, like Hoover, has become generic. The labelling machine will feed the continuous stationery, and cut it up into separate labels, gumming each one to a separately-fed cut form, or envelope, or whatever, and stacking the result.

**b) Self-adhesive labels**   These can be produced in any desired size and shape, with the backing paper fanfolded and provided with sprocket holes. The computer prints the labels, which can then be removed from the backing paper manually, or by a semi-automatic process, and stuck onto whatever medium.

**c) Computer letters**   In this variation either the entire computer letter, or the first sheet of each letter, is produced in continuous stationery form and fed through the computer printer, which adds the name and address, a salutation, and any other variable data in the text of the letter that the advertiser wishes to specify and that the list manager can program for. The letters will then proceed to a burster, or guillotine, where the fanfold will be separated into individual sheets, and the sprocket holes removed.

**d) Laser printing**   However, computer printers are slow, and highly inflexible, compared to a printing press. Typefaces are very limited as well. So the computer printer is normally limited to adding a few lines to each letter. An alternative to come on the scene in recent years is the laser printer (the ink-jet printer offers not dissimilar facilities from a different technical starting-point). Different models of laser printer will accept either continuous stationery or cut sheets, and will print on them *both* a standard text *and* individual variations (including of course name and address) in one pass, at speeds akin to those of a printing press rather than a line printer, and with a much extended range of typefaces. These printers are computer-driven, from magnetic tape, and a wide range of computer service bureaux now have such equipment, as well as the older line printers, which are now becoming outmoded so far as the production of promotion letters is concerned.

## 8   Lettershop

The lettershop, or mailing house, is the sharp end of the direct mail business, where the sins, delays, and other shortcomings of all the previous actors in the piece must either be made good, or inexorably come to light and start to exercise their baneful effect on the results of the mailing campaign. In the early days of the direct mail industry, the work of enclosing mailing material in envelopes was almost entirely manual, and tended to be handled on a piece-work, cottage industry basis. This mode of operation required very little working capital and incurred few overheads for the entrepreneur, and indeed a minimum of skills. This in turn led to a fiercely-competitive industry where margins were pared to the bone, and wages (or piece-rates) were held at very low levels: any departure from such a structure by one company would simply create a competitor under-cutting rates with the minimum of delay.

The availability of service houses working to tight margins had obvious short-term advantages for direct mail advertisers – and longer-term disadvantages as well. It was the cottage industry letter-shop business above all that helped to create for direct mail the undesirable public image of rat-faced exploiters squeezing little old ladies toiling by candlelight into the small hours to fulfil their quota of work for greedy capitalists. Worse still, the low cost of entry to the business encouraged the emergence of some dubious characters, who, finding that it was easier to get started in the business than greatly to prosper in it, turned to ways of improving their lot which were not within the rule-book, and sometimes not within the law, as we shall see.

Times have to a large extent changed. The advent of computer addressing has given a great boost to all forms of mechanical handling within the lettershop. This in turn has raised the ante for anyone who wishes to enter the lettershop game as a serious player. To date this has not resulted in the improvement one might expect in margins, and levels of wages: it is still easy, especially in a climate of heavy unemployment, to set up a small manual lettershop which can erode the business of its mechanized competitors. But this will change too. There is now a sufficiency of substantial, well-run, and properly conducted lettershops to satisfy the needs of direct mail advertisers; nevertheless advertisers, and their agents, need to be more aware than many have been in the past both of the constraints under which lettershops work, and of the damage that can be done to the prospects of a mailing if the work of the lettershop is not properly controlled and supervised.

The main functions of a mailing house are:

a) to receive the various items that constitute a single mailing from the various printers/manufacturers originating them;

b) to undertake such finishing tasks on each item as may not already have been performed – e.g. bursting of continuous station= ery, removal of sprocket holes, folding of items, etc.;

c) to collate the items required for the mailing and enclose these in the specified sequence in whatever type of enclosure material may be required;

d) where the items bearing names and addresses have been assem-bled in a particular sequence – e.g. for postal discount purposes

– to maintain that sequence through the various handling processes;

e) where two or more separate items in a mailing piece are individual to a particular customer (as for example where a name and address appears on one item, and an individual salutation on another) to ensure that items are correctly matched up in the enclosing process;

f) where addresses have been produced in no particular sequence, to sort mailing pieces prior to despatch to meet whatever Post Office requirements are laid down in order to achieve the level of postal discount agreed in advance with the advertiser or an agent;

g) to bag and label the final mailing pieces in accordance with Post Office requirements for the particular level of service agreed, and to arrange with the Post Office for collection;

h) to keep an accurate count of the number of pieces mailed, and to account for these to the Post Office, and to the advertiser or an agent;

i) to complete the task within the timespan agreed with the advertiser or an agent, and to provide documentary evidence that this has been done.

Enclosing may be in a conventional envelope, in a paper wrapper, or in plastic. In any of these modes, enclosing can be accomplished manually or by machine. Some items, by reason of their peculiar shape, or particularly unusual or complex make-up, may be unsuitable for mechanical handling, and therefore require manual enclosing. Where this is not the case, the interests of the advertiser are likely to be served by having the task performed by machine: there is a much better guarantee of a uniform result, and proper supervision is very much easier.

The particular type of mechanical equipment employed by the lettershop manager may have implications not only for work performance, and how much is to be charged for it, but also on events both precedent and subsequent to what happens within the lettershop itself. Let us consider an example. The most common form of enclosing machine in lettershop use is the Philipsburg. This Heath Robinson-looking machine has been chugging away inserting items in envelopes for as long as anyone in the industry can remember; other manufacturers have produced comparable equipment, sometimes with modest improvements, but the Philipsburg remains the workhorse of the lettershop business. However, this machine, once set up to do a particular job, performs exactly the same function on every cycle: that is to say, it picks up an item from each of its four, or six, stackers, collates them into the same sequence, inserts them into an envelope, seals it, and stacks it. Each envelope will contain exactly the same contents. Nowadays it is possible to obtain smart enclosing machines which will select material from a variety of different possible stackers, according to a coded instruction printed on each master document fed to the machine. In this way mailing pieces can be produced where the contents of each piece vary according to the particular needs of each addressee – the number of possible variations is, of course, not unlimited but the flexibility is substantial.

Consider the value of this in practice. An advertiser wishes to undertake a mailing to advertise a given product, but wishes, let us say, to test the effect of three different leaflets on prospects, without varying any other part of his mailing. If the mailing is to be enclosed on Philipsburgs, it will have to be split, prior to addressing, into three streams, corresponding to the three different leaflets to be used; each stream will be handled separately by the lettershop. This has two detrimental effects:

a) The computer installation that decided which addressee was to receive which leaflet, will have taken great care to ensure that names are randomly selected so that the response to the three leaflets can be properly compared. But unless scrupulous care is taken at the lettershop, it is probable that the three separate streams will be despatched in separate lots of mail sacks; what happens to them thereafter is largely a matter of chance, and it is quite probable that unintended – and untraceable – variations in handling by the postal system may contribute to an unknowable degree of variation in response between one stream and another, thus invalidating any conclusions that might be drawn from the test. One can actually see this happening again and again in observing direct mail results, where not only the quantity of response but actually the timing of response differs as between two or more test groups supposedly mailed at the same time, indicating either that the mailing house actually released them at different times, or that the Post Office treated them in some way differently. In order to avoid this outcome, the mailing house would require either to handle the three streams in parallel on three enclosing machines, mixing their outputs in common bags as they come off the lines, or else would have to wait until all three streams had completely enclosed (and mixed in the same bags) before any part of the mailing could be released. It is in practice totally improbable that any mailing house would do any such thing unless someone was standing over them the while – and even then the chances of error are substantial.

b) By splitting the mailing into three streams, it is possible, under the present rebate system, and almost certain under the new Mail-sort system, that the postal discount available for sortation will be smaller than it would be for a single stream.

Consider now what happens where the mailing house has a selective enclosing machine. First, the computer house does not have to divide the mailing into three and sort each stream separately; it will now sort one single stream, thereby saving some quantity of computer time. Instead, the computer will be programmed to put one of three codes in a predetermined spot on each addressed item. The enclosing machine will read this code, and enclose the appropriate leaflet, and other items, for each addressee, maintaining a single sorted stream. The mailing house can then put each bag into the post as its contents come off the enclosing line, secure in the knowledge that each bag contains a properly random mix of the three test leaflets. The advertiser will be able to believe the results of the test, and the postal discount available will be maximized.

Very few mailing houses have selective enclosing equipment. For this advertisers and advertising agencies are more to blame than the mailing houses themselves: the short-sighted emphasis of these people has all along been on keeping mailing costs to a minimum instead of ensuring an optimum service at a proper price. Here too the full-service house is best placed (or should be) to meet its clients' real needs, since it can objectively assess the relative merits of using a client's budget to tinker with copy, or to secure proper despatch arrangements. The advertiser who is not using a full-service house *must* have access to some person, either on the staff or employed as a consultant, who has an understanding of lettershop work, of the impact that its optimum performance ought to have on precedent operations, and of the need to pay a proper price for a proper job; past history suggests that advertising agencies that sub-contract lettershop work have neither the competence nor the incentive to deal with these issues in the way that the advertiser's interests demand.

Most lettershops have rather little opportunity to contribute "creatively" to the planning of a direct mail campaign, partly because there is a tendency among advertisers and agencies not to commission or consult lettershops until the planning is all complete, and partly because advertising agencies are frequently at pains to keep all their sub-contractors well away from their clients. Probably not many lettershops employ staff who are competent to make substantial contributions in this area (a chicken and egg problem), but this isn't always so. The best-known example to the contrary is the building (at The Lettershop in Leeds) of the Laserlope – a machine designed and built at a mailing house, to produce a highly-sophisticated type of mailing piece. The moral, which the industry has still not learned, is that the truly creative ideas which contribute to the success of a unique mailing may come from copy-writers, from designers, from list brokers, from computer staff (whose contributions we will be examining in the next section) and from mailing house staff. The task of constructing an optimum campaign demands that each of these disciplines has the opportunity – and is encouraged – to provide an input.

Having said which, most lettershops most of the time have to perform, quickly and efficiently, a fairly mundane function. In doing so, they have to take account of three parties: their client (who may be either an advertiser, or an agency acting on behalf of an advertiser), the printers or other suppliers from whom the materials on which they are to work must come, and the Post Office.

The lettershop's first concern in handling a mailing to meet the despatch date set by the client, is to ensure that the necessary materials are delivered on time, and in good condition. Clients, and agencies, find it very difficult to recognize that if a mailing consists of five pieces of material, and one of them is delivered late, the whole mailing, and not just 20% of it, will be delayed. Still less do they appreciate that the task of scheduling several different machine processes for a number of separate clients so as to make efficient use of machines in meeting scheduled dates, is a fairly complex exercise, where delays have a domino effect. There is a tendency among both advertisers and agencies to suppose that once the "creative" stage of a mailing is complete, and printers' proofs have been passed, the rest will happen automatically; progress-chasing tends to be non-existent, or desultory, resulting in last-minute panics where the lettershop is expected to make up for lost time by squeezing its schedules, working overtime, etc. Some delays, of course, are the fault of the lettershop itself, either directly, or indirectly because of fruitless efforts to make up for delays in an earlier job. Whichever way it happens, the result all too often is that the client (and/or the advertiser) receives a report about the despatch of his mailing which is, shall we say, less than the whole truth: mailings due out on a certain day will in fact go n days late, or part of the mailing will go on time, with the rest trailing after, or a mailing due to be spread over x days will actually spread over x + y days, with a full account of the situation often not being given – even where the lettershop is not itself at fault.

Untidy despatch of this kind might be expected to show up in a peculiar pattern of response – or indeed, where the mailing list has been "salted" with names of the advertiser's staff, in late arrival of the original mailing. In such circumstances there is a ready scapegoat to hand – the Post Office. Bulk mail these days is not normally post-marked, so there is no indication on the envelope of when it was received by the Post Office. Postal service is known to be both generally poor and subject to substantial fluctuations, both from time to time and from area to area; public perception of the service is even worse than the actuality. There is very little inclination, therefore, to question mailing house claims to have put material in the post on a certain date: the Post Office carries the blame for many peoples' faults besides its own.

Theoretically the answer to this problem is simple. The mailing house is required, for each posting, to fill in a postal docket (an official Post Office form) which forms the basis for postal accounting. The docket shows quantity of items posted at each weight step, and date of posting. The advertiser who is paying the cost of postage direct to the Post Office, should receive a copy of this docket from the Post Office to support the account. Where postage is being paid to the lettershop, leaving the latter to settle up with the Post Office, the advertiser *ought* to receive a copy of the postal docket from the lettershop, as part of the accounting process.

Alas in practice neither of these processes works too well. Many Post Offices are extremely slack in ensuring that they receive documentation completed properly and on time from lettershops. Dockets are frequently given to the Post Office late, particularly where a mailing has been spread over a number of days; the dates on them are unreliable, and the alleged quantities are rarely checked. Moreover, where the postage account is paid by the lettershop on behalf of the advertiser, it is the exception rather than the rule for the advertiser to receive a copy of the postal docket from the mailing house: this means there is no positive evidence that the mailing has taken place at all, or in the quantity alleged – leave alone that it has happened on a particular day.

Let us be quite clear. The great majority of mailing houses are scrupulously honest. But over the years there have been a small number – and still are – that are not. Without wishing to excuse dishonesty, it has to be said that this is mostly the fault of idle advertisers and agencies on the one side, and the Post Office on the other. Moreover, because opportunities for malpractice exist, the occurrence of an unexpectedly bad result on a mailing – a much more frequent happening than malpractice – will not infrequently result in an advertiser who has till then been reprehensibly slapdash, suddenly becoming paranoically suspicious. So let us consider just what are the opportunities for malfeasance in this area, and then ask what can be done to close them off.

a) The advertiser expects a mailing to be put in the post on a certain day, or spread in a given pattern over a number of days. The mailing house will be scheduling a number of activities for the same time-period, and the advertiser's activity may run late – either because some of the material was delivered late, or because some other activity was late, causing a domino effect on the schedule, or because the job took longer than anticipated – perhaps due to poor scheduling, perhaps due to imperfect material. Whatever the reason, the advertiser requires to know what posting(s) took place when. Sometimes a lettershop will indicate that a mailing went out on the required date, when in fact a small piece (or perhaps a large piece) of it went out subsequently; sometimes the advertising agency that has sub-contracted the mailing may be aware of the true situation, but less than anxious to admit the whole truth to the advertiser.

b) Most mailing houses will, if asked, handle postal accounting for the advertiser, and some, particularly among the smaller houses, are eager to do so. This is not surprising: lettershops in these circumstances request payment of postage (usually calculated on a gross, i.e. pre-discount, basis) x days in advance of the projected mailing date. They then stick this money in their bank account, where it accumulates interest (or is used as working capital) until the time comes to pay the Post Office, several weeks later. They then account to the advertiser for the net amount, returning any excess (or deducting it from their own bill for services). This accounting may, or may not, include copies of the official Post Office dockets (which may, or may not, have been stamped by the Post Office) apparently confirming that such-and-such a number of items of a certain weight were mailed on a certain day. Problems can occur. First, if the mailing house, between receiving the advertiser's money and completing the mailing, falls into the hands of the receiver, not only will the mailing not go out, but the postage paid in advance will become the property of the generality of the lettershop's creditors. Second, advertisers have no means of knowing whether or not the mailing was in fact despatched at all, whether in part or in whole, unless they receive a copy of the official, stamped, Post Office docket. (Even this is not a guarantee of the accuracy of the quantity mailed, but it is a guarantee that the lettershop will be invoiced by the Post Office for this quantity.) There are certainly cases of lettershops performing half of an advertiser's mailing, docketing that half and paying the Post Office for it, meanwhile pocketing the advertiser's money intended to pay for postage on the other half. Advertisers who are dozy enough to facilitate such a state of affairs deserve, in a certain sense, what they get. Unfortunately, the industry as a whole pays, since the response to such a campaign will only be half of what it should have been, and the advertiser will, even if suspicions remain dormant, be disappointed with the results.

c) It isn't only the advertiser that can be ripped off by the occasional unscrupulous lettershop: the Post Office too may suffer. The lettershop may take the correct money for postage from the advertiser, and indeed mail correctly – but make out postal dockets (which they know the advertiser will not see) for smaller quantities than are actually mailed, resulting in smaller postal bills, and a surplus for the lettershop. There is always a risk that the Post Office will execute a random check of such a mailing, and discover a discrepancy; against this there are two defences. First, check weighings (all that the Post Office can be reasonably expected to do) cannot give an answer accurate within 15%; there is little risk for a lettershop in ripping off the Post Office for, say, 10% of postage on a large mailing – provided the advertiser is not going to see the postal docket. Second, even if the lettershop is greedier than 15%, most Post Offices on discovering such a discrepancy will simply phone up the offender and point out that a mistake has been made; the lettershop will apologise profusely, and correct it – this time.

So, what can be done to enable the advertiser to safeguard against the effects of this kind of villainy? Really, all that is required is that both advertisers and the Post Office should exercise the sort of vigilance in this field that most businessmen regard as second nature in other areas, such as receipt of goods. For example:

i) An increasing number of advertisers are nowadays opening direct accounts with the Post Office, rather than paying for their mailings through a mailing house. Particularly for large advertisers, who may use a number of mailing houses, as well, possibly, as undertaking substantial amounts of mailing on their own accounts, this has numerous advantages, not least being the consolidation of total postage bills under a single account. It does also eliminate the temptation for a mailing house to be less than 100per cent above-board in terms of postage paid, quantities mailed, and discounts earned.

ii) Mailsort will bring with it new docketing procedures, which will in principle be much harder to cheat on; the Post Office intends in addition to have more frequent and tighter checks on dates, weights and quantities. But above all, those advertisers, who will now be paying their bills to the Post Office, will get copies of the dockets that form the basis of their payments.

iii) Advertisers need to insist that arrangements with lettershops, whether made by themselves, or by agencies on their behalf, are fully documented. In fairness to both parties, this means that the lettershop's obligation to mail on or by a given date must be balanced by an assurance of supply of materials by an agreed date. Advertisers should then insist on having the opportunity to inspect the lettershop's work while in progress, and to receive precise notification of completion. If advertisers are prepared to exercise oversight of the mailing process themselves, well and good. If they feel they can trust an advertising agency to do so on their behalf, equally OK. But if they are employing a direct marketing consultant, this is a task that functionary would automatically expect to perform.

iv) Above all, advertisers and agencies need to stop treating lettershop work as though it were some tedious afterthought to the creative process of inventing a mailing. A good lettershop can be a valuable partner in the creative process; over and above that, it has a serious job to perform, which, according to whether it is done well or badly, honestly or less so, will affect the results of the campaign – very possibly to a much greater extent than anything a "creative" agency can, for good or ill, achieve.

## 9 Fulfilment

Some further definition of terms may be called for here. Whereas the lettershop work we have been discussing consists in enabling an advertiser to get direct mail advertising material into the post, en route to the potential customers' letter boxes, fulfilment work consists in handling customer-generated response to advertisers' messages. This can take a whole variety of forms: consumers sending in six Brand X box-tops, who must be sent a plastic daffodil, or £1 sterling, or a clutch of discount coupons, in exchange; people applying for free samples of this or that product; people seeking further and fuller particulars of such and such an offer; people ordering, and perhaps sending money, or credit-card details, for an advertised product.

Some lettershops will undertake fulfilment work also, although rather few of them specialize in this type of activity; at all events we will discuss fulfilment houses as though they were – as indeed many are – a separate phenomenon. The basic requirements for running a successful fulfilment house are first of all warehousing capacity for whatever items clients may wish to despatch to those responding to their offers, and secondly a highly flexible labour force able to adapt itself to every manner of odd requirement. Nowadays a further requirement is computer equipment which can be used to capture names and addresses and to print labels that will carry the fulfiment packs to their appointed destinations.

This thought raises a curious reflection. Many fulfilment houses handle hundreds of thousands of consumer names and addresses each week – a high proportion of them arising from responses to point-of-sale offers for fmcg items. Most of these names and addresses are data-captured – as the simplest way of initiating the fulfilment process. Yet enormous numbers of these names, captured on a computer and recorded on disk, are never again used by the companies concerned, many of whom, if they have heard of such things as databases and direct marketing at all, are quite convinced these have no connection with their business.

Those who have persevered with us thus far will recognize this as the most terrible heresy of all: at a time when companies alive to the direct marketing process are straining every nerve to accumulate relevant data, it is a shock to find marketing dinosaurs (and many of them are giants in point of size, as well as in evident lack of cranial capacity) who blithely ignore or discard data that has already been captured.

Be that as it may, the advertiser who seeks a fulfilment house should look for one that is capturing data on computer as a matter of course, thus acquiring, as a by-product of the fulfilment operation, a quantity of valuable data. If the list can't be used in a further marketing effort, then at the very least it is a marketable asset which through a list broker can earn revenue.

Commissioning a fulfilment operation demands the same kind of common-sense vigilance required in commissioning a lettershop: the advertiser needs to have proper evidence that instructions have been carried out fully, and in a timely manner. In practice far too much of this work is done sloppily – and once again this is primarily the fault of the advertiser, or the agency. This is particularly true of point-of-sale offers, where the main object of the campaign is to stimulate sales of the brand, and fulfilment of the "special offer" is seen as a side issue, to be farmed out and forgotten about.

Of course, where fulfilment is in consequence of a request from a consumer, who is therefore expecting something, failure by the fulfilment house to execute its instructions in any significant number of cases is likely to give rise to a large body of complaint to the advertiser, who will thus be alerted to the problem. Nonetheless, advertisers should, as a matter of course, set up a regular reporting structure which will enable them to know daily how many requests for fulfilment have arrived, how many have been handled, how many have been posted (supported by Post Office documentation) and how many are awaiting action. And they should inspect the activities of their chosen fulfilment house from time to time, either in person, or through an agency or consultant.

## 10  Computer Bureaux

In the context of the kind of activities dealt with in this book, a company may have cause to consider using a computer bureau in any of the following circumstances:

> as a list manager, as described in Section 4 above on The List Business;

> to build a database system, which may subsequently be run on the client's own computer in-house, or by the bureau;

> to run a database system.

**a) List management**  List management is a function required by list owners either because they are making more or less frequent use of the list themselves, and require it kept up to date for that purpose, or because they wish to derive a subsidiary income from renting the list to other users, and need, through list maintenance, to preserve the quality of this marketable asset. We will examine one or two possible scenarios, to determine in the case of each what might be the advantages to list owners of using a computer bureau.

> i) Consider first the fmcg manufacturer referred to briefly in the previous section on Fulfilment. He acquires names and addresses as a result of his point-of-sale activities, and uses a fulfilment

house to carry out his obligations to those persons. As a by-product of this operation he has a continuing flow of computerized consumer addresses, with a certain amount of data about each – but at this time no further use for this data in the context of his own operation. Such a person will require to find a list broker who will market the list, and a list manager (quite possibly the same person) who will maintain it on a computer, make parts of it available to clients as required, and update it in respect of any new data acquired – including, for example, "gone away" information resulting from mailings. For manufacturers to perform these chores for themselves would probably make little sense, diverting them from their true business into areas in which they have little experience or skill, and in which potential earnings would be a quite small proportion of their business interests. Use in such a case of outside bureau services, which provide list owners with a continuing revenue for little on-going effort, makes excellent sense.

Nonetheless, certain precautions do have to be taken. List owners will probably wish to specify certain restrictions as to the kinds of business to which the list can, or cannot, be rented – to exclude direct competitors, for example. They should expect to receive from the list broker each month a list of all companies who have contracted to rent the list, and they will wish either themselves, or the broker on their behalf, to have advance sight of all material it is proposed to mail to names from their list. If the broker is to exercise this oversight, a set of criteria will need to be supplied by which material can be judged to be suitable or not. And finally, list owners will wish to "salt" their lists with a sprinkling of names and addresses which, by virtue of their spelling, use of initials, or some such, are instantly recognizable by their recipients as having emanated from a particular list. Such persons, on receiving a promotion from the list, will send it to a single person in the list owner's organization, who will be able to spot any unauthorized, or otherwise unsuitable, use of the list. (It is also important that all those involved – the list broker, list manager, and indeed the list owner's own staff, all know that the list has been salted in this way – prevention is always better than cure.)

ii) Next, take the case of a small magazine publisher who has a list of subscribers which is used regularly for the despatch of copies, and for sending out renewal notices and bills. But this is regarded as a fairly mechanical small-scale chore; just as the printing, binding, and wrapping of the publication are sub-contracted, so the publisher feels that it would make sense to contract out also the addressing, despatch and list maintenance functions, which otherwise represent a distraction from the actual job of publishing the magazine. And if this contracted job can be handled by a company that can also earn some revenue for the publisher by renting use of the list to non-competitive advertisers, so much the better for everyone.

iii) The company which is using its list of past customers as an integral part of its day-to-day marketing effort, cross-promoting product x to buyers of product y, is in a somewhat different position. The list – or, as surely it should in such a case become, the database – is now so central a part of the operation of this company that it is to be expected that most such operators would wish to have it managed on their own computer in-house, where it can be instantly accessed, and where the company's own staff is available to react swiftly to the changing needs of the moment. But how, in such a company, does the database come to be created in the first place?

**b) Creating a database**   The use of computers in business and industry is today widespread; few companies of any size do not have computer equipment of some kind, and substantial installations of hardware, supported by systems and operating staff, are a commonplace. Why, in these circumstances, is there still such a thriving business for computer service bureaux? And why are these bureaux occupied, for much of their time, in working for clients who already have their own, often large, computer installations?

Two reasons can be found for this curious state of affairs. First, most computer staff are neither intelligible to, nor understanding of, the businesses in which they work, and by which they are paid. There is an enormous gulf of understanding, in most computerized companies, between the professional systems staff, who have a limited understanding of what the business is about, and little or no feel for how the individual talents within it actually operate, and the company's general management, who, despite familiarization sessions, have no gut feeling for what a computer can and cannot do, or which types of problem are simple and which difficult for a computer to handle.

Second, every computer department, regardless of size, is always full up with work, now and for the next six months. (Although I have been a computer manager myself for some years, and experienced this phenomenon close to, I am far from clear as to the reasons for it, so I give none: I offer the observation merely as an extension of Parkinson's Law, and other such mysterious forces, like gravity, whose effects one can measure without having the slightest notion of their causes.) This means that any manager requiring systems work, whether in the form of a few hours' work, or a major project, must submit the demand to some type of evaluation system, which will either give it priority on the grounds of perceived urgency, or, more probably, will assign it to the back of the queue, to be started six months hence – always provided its place is not in the interim usurped by something more evidently important.

Faced with this dual problem, of poor communications and inaccessability of resources, marketing directors who have become convinced of the need to capture and maintain all the information they can about their customers, their prospects, their behaviour, life styles, and all that – and who see this information daily escaping for want of any system of data-capture – will be attracted by the idea of going to an outside bureau. This will give them access to people whose very livelihood depends on being able to communicate intelligibly, and who, if they choose their bureau carefully, have some experience in the database field, which their own internal computer staff probably do not.

There is no single answer to the question whether this is a sensible move or not. What we can do is to consider what is the necessary – or at any rate the desirable – relationship between the marketing staff for whose immediate use the database must be designed, and the systems staff who must create it. Each marketing director must then make up his/her own mind whether this kind of relationship can be created – and the work done within the required timescale – with existing company resources, or whether he/she needs to look outside.

The most often-reiterated statement of the proper relationship between computer technician and computer user is that users must define their requirements, which it is then up to the technician to find an appropriate means of meeting. This is the most awful piece of rubbish, which has been responsible for a high proportion of the disasters that have occurred in the computer world over the last thirty years. Most aspiring computer users don't have "requirements" in this sense at all – first and foremost they have problems, which usually fill their horizons; secondly, when they do get a little breathing space, they have dreams, aspirations, concepts even – but requirements, no. A statement of requirements implies a prior analysis of problems, and indeed a determination of the broad means by which they should be solved. In fact computer users have no idea, initially, which of their aspirations are practical or impractical, easy or difficult, cheap or expensive. The ends one wishes to achieve, and the means of achieving them are simply not separable, in systems analysis any more than in philosophy.

Further, few computer users, and particularly few marketers, have the *kind* of mental equipment, or training, or inclination that would enable them to undertake a rigorous analysis on which a statement of requirements could be based – even if they had a sufficient background understanding of the technical possibilities to render this fruitful. In fact, when one hears a computer manager demanding that a prospective user should produce a clear written statement of requirements, this is normally a cop-out: the computer manager knows that no such statement will be forthcoming; if, however, a statement is presented, the manager will find twenty-six questions to ask about the statement, and another twenty-six about each of the answers – this will keep things ticking over fairly indefinitely, and will postpone the evil day when it has to be admitted that the resources to embark on the task at any time during the next six months are lacking.

Producing a statement of requirements is a task for systems analysts. It is moreover a wholly crucial task. It can be divided, conceptually, into four parts. First, analysts must get to understand the way in which the part of the organization they are looking at now functions; they must understand this in the fullest possible detail. Much of that detail will turn out to be peripheral, and will be discarded from further consideration, but some – and it is impossible to tell which in advance – may prove crucial, so everything must be absorbed in this first phase. Second, analysts must be able to reduce the mass of material so acquired to essentials; they must be able to describe the current functioning of the entity analysed with just enough detail to render it intelligible. Third, they must be able to reconstruct this entity on paper, in a way which will minimize existing problems, and maximize opportunities, within the accepted constraints of the function itself. To do this properly, they will have to stand inside the mind of the user, and to sense problems and opportunities as the user does, only with greater clarity. Fourthly, and most importantly of all, they must not only sell this system re-design to those who will operate it; they must actually convince them that all the important parts of it were their idea in the first place. Then, and only then, can the task of implementing the system begin.

Of course, the process is nothing like as simple a series of events as the above suggests: for a start the whole procedure is iterative rather than simply serial. That is to say, the tasks of learning current procedures and reducing what one learns to essentials go on in parallel: one's "essential model" is modified – sometimes wholly reconstructed – in the light of each new finding. Again, reconstruction is not a single uninterrupted process: each step of the process must be tested in dialogue with the user, and modified in the light of his/her comments; in this way the process of "selling" the ultimate design is a continuing one, interwoven with the design process itself.

A company that has a computer systems department dedicated to this type of approach, and possessed of analysts capable of carrying it through, should not have to look to an external bureau to construct its marketing database – subject, of course, to the problem of priorities already alluded to. But a company where the systems department has no spare capacity, or where the systems manager seeks to conceal problems by asking for a statement of requirements, will be one whose marketing director would be well advised to see what external assistance can be acquired.

**c) Running a database**   Only a few years ago, creating, maintaining, and running a marketing database would have been regarded as a major undertaking not only in terms of systems development (which it still is) but in terms of hardware requirements. Today this is much less true, and concern that such a development would cause overload on existing computer hardware, or necessitate acquisition of extensive further hardware, expensive both intrinsically and in terms of space, maintenance, operating, etc., can be largely discounted. Indeed, there are already two or three software offerings available in this country that enable quite large databases (say of up to 200,000 persons) to be run on a microcomputer with a hardware cost of less than £5,000. And indeed these software packages are such that, once the system is designed and installed, technical computer considerations are almost non-existent, and the whole process of interrogating and using the database can be handled by the end-user – the marketing director and staff, sitting at their own desks.

This state of affairs has greatly lessened the case for using a bureau actually to hold and operate one's database, and increased the case for putting computer power at the finger-tips of the end-user, rather than centralizing it in either a computer department or an external bureau. However, there remain two problems – bulk printing from the database, and data maintenance. As to the printing problem, microcomputers will not at this date support fast line printers, or continuous stationery laser printers, such as are necessary for volume printing; a means therefore has to be available for transferring data in magnetic medium to a location where adequate printing capacity is available.

The second problem is somewhat harder, although it depends on the type of database in use, and the extent of new data affecting it. One thing is for sure: the marketing director may be very glad to be able to call individual items from a database to a screen in the office, and to initiate analyses or manipulations, or print-outs of the data at the touch of a button – but is not likely to relish the thought of having to handle large volumes of data consisting of changes of address, "gone away" notifications, orders, cancellations, payments, and all the other multifarious items that can impact the database. For this reason, a compromise solution may make sense, under which the database is held, and maintained, at a central location possessed of the facilities to handle all the updating chores, while the marketing department can access the database directly from one or more micros of its own, with facilities to download all or part of the database onto that micro, and there to handle it as may be required.

## 11   Conclusions

For those about to make their first essay into database marketing, as for those with a dawning interest in direct mail, there is a plethora of agencies of all kinds waiting to lend a hand (and to take their money). The object of this chapter has been to indicate the kinds of service that are available, the sort of circumstances that would indicate resort to each, and the pros and cons of this or that alternative. The chapter that follows attempts to indicate the sources of further information that are available, in terms of organizations, of listings, and of reading materials. What cannot be done (entertaining though it might be) is to indicate the strengths and weaknesses, skill or lack of it, of this or that operator. So, use these sources to determine what sort of facilities are available from whom; when it comes to choosing which outfit to select you are on your own – unless, that is to say, you have a good consultant at your elbow to help in choosing.

# 9  Other Information Sources

1. *Direct Mail Services Standards Board (DMSSB)*  This body was set up, with Post Office funding, in 1983. Its objective is 'to encourage the achievement and maintenance of the highest standards of practice and conduct in the direct mail services industry'. To this end it runs a recognition scheme for direct mail service houses of all kinds, and publishes a list of recognized houses (currently over 150 of them). There are still an awful lot of companies offering services in direct mail (including database facilities) that are not recognized by the Board. However, most of the major players are recognized, and anyone contemplating buying services from an un-recognized house should, for their own protection, satisfy themselves of the reasons for such non-recognition.

   The strength of the Board as a source of advice is that it is an independent body, beholden to no one. It is run on a day-to-day basis by a Chief Executive (Mr Michael Goodrich) and an Assistant Director (Miss Priscilla Titford). Its governing body is a Council (whose Chairman is Mrs Kate Foss) composed of prominent members of the industry, and independent persons. The Board has always worked closely with the Advertising Standards Authority. At the time of writing it appears that this relationship may shortly become a much more formalized one, with the Board becoming an arm of the Authority. Meanwhile, its address is:

   DMSSB
   26 Eccleston Street
   London SW1W 9PY
   Tel: (01) 824-8651

2. *Trade Associations*  One of the major weaknesses of the direct marketing industry in the UK is the plethora of overlapping trade associations it contains. Attempts have been made to rationalize the situation – so far unsuccessfully. From the viewpoint of the direct mail user this doesn't matter too much – so long as he can distinguish who does what.

a) *British Direct Marketing Association (BDMA)* This is much the largest of the trade associations. In a rational world it would in fact be the spokesman for the industry as a whole, with other specialist bodies, that represent segments of the industry, operating under its umbrella. The BDMA's weakness in the past has arisen from an inability wholly to reconcile the conflicting interests of its different groups of members – who include both advertisers (or traders as the Association quaintly calls them) and suppliers of services to advertisers. The Association has become a much more credible body since the appointment of a professional full-time Director (Mr. Colin Fricker). The continuation of the industry's fragmentation is now a reflection not so much of the inadequacy of the BDMA (as was originally the case) as of the inertia of the status quo. The Association's address is:

BDMA
Grosvenor Gardens House
Grosvenor Gardens
London SW1W 0BS
Tel: (01) 630-7322

b) *Direct Mail Producers' Association (DMPA)* Originally an Association of mailing houses, or lettershops, who did not feel that the BDMA as then constituted dealt adequately with their particular interests. The Association now includes a number of other service houses – notably direct mail agencies. Nor does it admit just anyone: applicants for membership must have been trading for at least two years, and are then thoroughly vetted. Naturally enough the Association will not recommend one of its members as against others, but it can be of assistance in finding one's way around. The Director of the Association is Mr. Mark Elwes, and its address is:

DMPA
34 Grand Avenue
London N10 3BP
Tel: (01) 883 9854

c) *British List Brokers' Association (BLBA)* This is a relatively new body, in the area of direct marketing that most needs attention to standards. There are not many list brokers, so the Association is small. It has produced a code of practice for its members, some of whom are vigorously seeking to introduce a more professional approach to this arm of the business. The Association has no full-time Director (a distinct weakness); its Chairman at the time of writing is Mr. Graham Jenner, who is to be found at:

BLBA
c/o Springfield House
West Street
Bedminster
Bristol BS3 3NX
Tel: (0272) 666900

d) *Promotion Handlers' Association (PHA)*  This is the latest of the trade associations to be formed; it consists of companies with a substantial interest in fulfilment work – the handling, that is, of coupon response from advertisements. The Chairman of the PHA at the time of writing (there is no full-time staff) is Mr Alan Crossman, who may be found at:

PHA
c/o Mailcom plc
Snowdon Drive
Winterhill
Milton Keynes MK6 1HQ
Tel: (0908) 675666

3. *Direct Mail Sales Bureau (DMSB)*  This organization was set up in 1982 by the Post Office, together with a number of service houses, with the object of selling the use of direct mail to advertising agencies and their clients. The Bureau, that is to say, acts as a central point of reference for those wishing to buy services in this field. It is a commercial organization, seeking to earn a profit, and its first aim, other things being equal, will be to sell the services of its shareholders. Its Chairman is Michael Manton; its full-time Managing Director is:

Frank MacGinty
DMSB
14 Floral Street
London WC2E 9RR
Tel: (01) 379-7531

4. *Mailing Preference Service (MPS)*  This body was also set up with Post Office help in 1982. Its object was to enable consumers

to register with a single body their desire to receive, or not to receive, direct mail advertising of particular kinds – i.e. in particular to act as a safety-valve for disgruntled consumers. The service collects details of all consumers who write to it, and forwards these, in computerized media, to its subscribers. It is extremely important to the health and reputation of the industry that all those who own consumer mailing lists should subscribe to, and use the facilities of, the MPS. It is also highly desirable that advertisers should only use lists that are regularly 'cleaned' against MPS lists; it may shortly become mandatory on list brokers to ensure this in respect of any consumer lists that they broke. The Chairman of MPS at time of writing is Paddy Cribb, of Freemans. Its full-time Chief Executive is:

Kay Beckett
MPS
26 Eccleston Street
London SW1W 9PY
Tel: (01) 730 0844

5. *Data Protection Registrar*   The duty of this personage is to ensure compliance with the Data Protection Act, which has been dealt with at length above (Chapter 5 Section 2). The present incumbent is:

Eric Howe
Office of the Data Protection Registrar
Springfield House
Water Lane
Wilmslow
Cheshire
Tel: (0625) 535777

6. *The Royal Mail*   Direct mail is the fastest growing component of letter traffic handled by the Royal Mail. For this very sufficient reason, the Royal Mail is eager to act in concert with – indeed as part of – the direct mail industry. A number of schemes are available for the assistance of direct mail users; those not well-acquainted with them already can find out more from the Marketing Department of Royal Mail Letters, which may be found at:

Royal Mail Marketing
33 Grosvenor Place
London SW1X 1PX
Tel: (01) 235-8000

7. *Listings* Nobody has yet succeeded (although several have tried) in producing a wholly comprehensive and effective guide to direct marketing services. The latest, and most nearly comprehensive entrant is British Rate and Data with *Brad Direct Marketing*. This consists of a list of mailing lists available for rental, and a list of companies offering services of all kinds, with appropriate indices. It is compiled by Mardev, itself a notable player in the list-broking game. The first edition was published in September 1988, and it is the best of its kind to date. However, the list of service companies in particular is still not comprehensive; the data given on each company is sparse to say the least, and the index categorizing their various activities is not user-friendly. No doubt it will improve with practice.

Earlier ventures in this field include the *Direct Mail Databook*, published by Gower Press. The fifth edition came out in 1987, and is for all practical purposes superseded by Brad. (Benn Publications had an early entry in the field, *Direct Marketing Services*, published in 1980.)

From time to time *Direct Response Magazine* publishes a booklet giving details of companies offering services in this or that capacity. The information given in these listings is substantially greater than in Brad (or Gower), and they are therefore useful. The difficulty with these booklets, is firstly that they are very far indeed from being comprehensive, and secondly that the description of each company's facilities is written by the company, which imparts a variable degree of credibility – or sometimes intelligibility – to each.

8. *Bibliography* Useful books on direct marketing, or on database, are not numerous; books that you can actually *read*, without going to sleep, are few and far between. The traditional direct marketing picture has been one of a number of heavyweight American tomes, some of which contain valuable material if one knows where to find it, but all of which are so totally indigestible as to render their practical value of considerable doubt. British books have been in shorter supply, and have avoided the temptation to give encyclopaedic coverage to what is, after all, a potentially immense subject. The British are catching up now in the numbers game, and thankfully have not forgotten that books are there to be read, not simply to provide impressive office furniture.

8.1 *American books* Let us start with the blockbusters:

Baier, Martin *Elements of Direct Marketing*, McGraw Hill, 1984. (Also in paperback)

Hodgson, Richard S. *Dartnell Direct Mail & Mail Order Handbook,* Dartnell Corporation, 3rd edn, 1980

Kobs, Jim *Profitable Direct Marketing,* Crain Books, 1980

Nash, Edward (ed.) *The Direct Marketing Handbook,* McGraw Hill, 1984. (A collection of articles by leading US practitioners.)

Nash, Edward L. *Direct Marketing: Strategy – Planning – Execution,* McGraw Hill, 2nd edn, 1986

Stone, Bob *Successful Direct Marketing Methods,* Crain Books, 3rd edn, 1984

Then there are a number of American books that I would describe as primarily academic studies:

Cohen, W. *Response Marketing,* Wiley, 1984

Ljungren, *The Business-to-Business Direct Marketing Handbook,* Amacom, 1989

Retzler, K. *Direct Marketing,* Scott Foresman, 1988. (I rather gave up on this one when I discovered that one of the chapters was entitled 'Choosing a Media': this I feel disqualifies the author, and publisher, from being allowed access to any form of writing materials, for any purpose.)

And a few recent American titles that are perhaps rather less hard going, and less bludgeoningly didactic, than their predecessors:

Graham & Jones *Selling by Direct Mail,* Piatkus, 1985

Holtz *The Direct Marketer's Workbook,* Wiley, 1986

Roman, Ernan *Integrated Direct Marketing,* McGraw Hill, 1988

Weintz, Walter *The Solid Gold Mailbox,* Wiley, 1987. (An anecdotal book, for those that like that sort of thing, about successful direct mail campaigns. Personally I always feel there is much more to be learned from failures than from successes, but people are strangely reluctant to write about these.)

And one hybrid book composed of articles by American and European practitioners:

Dillon, J. (ed.) *Handbook of International Direct Marketing,* McGraw Hill, 1976

8.2 *British books*  Still few on the ground, but with some note-worthy recent additions. None of them will break your wrist, and some of them are actually interesting:

Andrews, Les (ed.) *Direct Mail Handbook,* for The Royal Mail, Exley, 2nd edn, 1989. (A collection of articles by leading UK practitioners; a very useful introduction.)

Bird, Drayton *Commonsense Direct Marketing,*Kogan Page, 2nd edn, 1989. (A succinct, frequently witty, book by one of the industry's foremost copy-writers.)

Brann, Christian *Cost Effective Direct Marketing,* Collectors Books, 1984. (The author has now retired from his eponymous company, but is still one of the best lecturers on the circuit, particularly on the fundamentals of the business. This is an ideal introductory book.)

Fairlie, Robin *Direct Mail: Principles and Practice,* Kogan Page, 1979

Fraser Robinson, John *The Secrets of Effective Direct Mail,* McGraw Hill, 1989. (Essential reading.)

Jones, J.A. *Databases in Theory and Practice,* Kogan Page, 1986. (A good deal stronger on theory than practice, but a good theoretical introduction.)

Shaw & Stone *Database Marketing,* Gower, 1988

# Index